# GREEN

*A practical A-Z guide
to your garden —
tips, crafts, recipes & remedies*

# THUMBS

# GREEN

A practical A-Z guide
to your garden ~
tips, crafts, recipes & remedies

# THUMBS

## Pamela Allardice

BayBooks
An imprint of HarperCollins*Publishers*

A Bay Books Publication
An imprint of HarperCollinsPublishers

First published in Australia in 1994 by Bay Books

Bay Books, of
HarperCollinsPublishers Pty Limited
25-31 Ryde Road, Pymble NSW 2073, Australia

HarperCollinsPublishers (New Zealand) Limited
31 View Road, Glenfield, Auckland 10, New Zealand

HarperCollinsPublishers Limited
77-85 Fulham Palace Road, London W6 8JB, United Kingdom

National Library of Australia
Cataloguing-in-Publication data:
Allardice, Pamela, 1958–
Green thumbs.
ISBN 1 86378 180 3.
1. Gardening — Miscellaneous. 2. Gardening — Quotations,
maxims, etc. I. Title.
635

Printed in Australia by The Griffin Press, Adelaide.
Cover illustration Kate Mitchell

9 8 7 6 5 4 3 2 1

97  96  95  94

'The people one meets as one travels along the garden path are delightful, remarkably generous and invariably genuine. Their eyes are bright, their faces bronzed, their hands are full of callouses, and their hearts are brimming over with the love of plants.'

HELEN MORGENTHAU FOX

(quoted in *The Scented Garden* by Louise Beebe Wilder, Dover Publications, New York, 1974)

# INTRODUCTION

The ability—or inability—to make plants thrive has been recognised by many. 'Green thumbs' are no respecters of persons, either. In New Delhi a number of years ago, Prince Charles observed two trees planted previously by his parents and noted that his mother's tree, though younger, was taller. His comment: 'The trees that my mother plants always do well, but not those planted by my father.'

Everything grows in my mother's garden, too. There are daffodils with magnificent golden trumpets like Gabriel's horn, tulips with blossoms like brandy snifters and a dwarf (hah) buddleia, with beautifully scented, pure white blossoms, which are lovely if you can see them without tipping over backwards. Not to mention her sweetpeas, petunias, gardenias, tomatoes, radishes, night-scented cactus, bush orchids, fuchsias and fruit trees.

Not only does everything grow in my mother's garden, everything *grows*. After a week away, you have to slash your way through giant hollyhocks and great sprays of old-fashioned pink roses just to reach the front door, much as Prince Charming must have done *en route* to the Sleeping Beauty. In spring, you can pick enormous armfuls of bluebells and wallflowers. In summer, bees put on a disgraceful Bacchanalian display. So drunk are they on nectar from the luscious red roses that they lurch into one another. Even in winter, my mother's garden is replete with colour and fragrance.

Not only do her flowers and herbs give visual pleasure, they may also be put to numerous uses around the house. The simplest food can be greatly enhanced by the flavours of a few carefully-chosen herbs. Leaves and flowers can be pressed and used to decorate candles, greeting cards and placemats. Scented blossoms add fragrance to pretty pillows, while herbs and flowers combine in effective beauty products, just like those your mother might have made, or her mother before her.

Much has been written about why some people are successful gardeners and others are not. Russell Page, in *The Education of a Gardener*, said, 'Green fingers are the extension of a verdant heart.'

He believed good gardens could be made only by gardeners who understood plants in a very real sense. With his own wide-ranging interests spanning French, Italian, Japanese and English landscaping, he added, with some humility, 'I never saw a garden from which I did not learn something'.

Luther Burbank, a well-respected plant breeder, was known to fellow horticulturalists as 'the plant wizard', for having developed and introduced nearly 1000 new varieties of flowers, fruit and vegetables during the 19th century. He believed love was a vital source of nourishment. He assured his plants of his appreciation and always asked for their help in producing the many new strains he was famous for. Towards the end of his life, Burbank wrote, 'What a joy life is when you have made a close working relationship with Nature.' Julia S. Berrall makes a similar point when she says, 'Lastly, always love your flowers. By some subtle sense the dear things always detect their friends and, for them, they will live longer and bloom more freely than they ever will for a stranger.'

So, what are the secrets of my mother's 'green thumb'? Does she favour chook poo? Eye of bat and toe of frog? Midnight watering sprees? Perhaps a special planting incantation or blessing? Or lucky secateurs?

Mum is kneeling, weeding, and rises to greet me, brushing dirt from her hands on her old gardening pants.

'Secret?' she says, absently, in response to my question. 'There's no great secret to gardening. I guess it's like most things—you get out of it what you put in.'

Well, I know what I want out of life. I want my children to say, 'My mother's got green thumbs.'

# CREATING YOUR OWN MAGIC

Through time, many gardeners have indulged a fancy for improving their crops with a little white—or 'green'—magic. What, you say, have flowers and herbs got to do with spooks and spells? Rather a lot. If you're of a superstitious nature, sow wisely. It is said that certain plants are lucky to have around the house and that others should be carefully avoided. The trick is, apparently, to encourage the beneficial ones to grow in your garden by planting them at the time of the full moon ...

Recent research has brought a lot of these age-old beliefs about the 'personality' of plants, their cultivation, their medicinal uses and even their links with human life into fresh prominence. Confirmed by eyewitnesses since earliest times, life indices, communication between plants, or between plants and humans, and the ability of plants to reveal events, not to mention oddball ideas to enhance their growth and flowering or fruiting behaviour, are all now being investigated.

Perhaps the growing belief in the relationship between plants and people points to a desire deeper than the mere preservation of a species; to a more primitive emotion, a desire to draw nearer to Nature herself. While nurserymen do not suggest that their seed mixtures will conciliate the Great Goddess, such plantings will undoubtedly create gardens favourable for the reception of nature spirits, or *devas*. Maybe, after all, gardeners with 'green thumbs' who favour a little propitiatory magic and ecologists are really talking about the same thing.

Recipes and household hints passed from one generation to the next are often the best you can get, so plenty are included in the book. Even the most simple garden can be a constant source of delight when one knows how to harvest it.

If your thumb could do with some greening, read on!

## ALOE VERA

Cosmetic manufacturers have been quick to include aloe vera extract in shampoos, moisturisers and sunscreens. However, its uses as a remedy for skin disorders such as insect bites, scratches and burns, are not new. Aloe plants were well known to physicians in ancient Greece and Rome. In much the same way as it may be applied to heal burns and bites in people, aloe vera juice (or gel) can be applied to a lopped or broken tree branch. The benefits are twofold. The gel will help heal the injury more rapidly and its bitter taste will repel any predators which might attack the exposed area of the plant.

Aloe also has a long history of use as a purgative and tonic, both for human and for veterinary purposes. Even today, old-style farmers in the American Ozarks will toss a cut leaf into their chickens' drinking trough, saying this will clear them of any parasites.

*See also Hands*

## ANTS

In ancient China, certain species of ants were especially placed in citrus orchards because they attacked cater-pillars. Slim bamboo runways were actually strung between trees to facilitate their transit. In the main, however, ants are not so popular, due to their habit of spreading aphids and mealybugs

throughout the garden. Discourage them by planting a patch of tansy or mint. If completely exasperated, spray their nest with garlic and white pepper.

*See also Catnip*

## ANT BITES

Some people are quite allergic to ant bites. If you are a victim of an ant attack and find the bite starts to swell alarmingly, try massaging the affected area with vitamin E cream, or pierce a vitamin E capsule and use the high-potency oil inside. This will help reduce pain, itching and swelling, without any of the side effects of the cortisone-based, anti-inflammatory creams usually prescribed for such allergic reactions.

*See also Nettles*

EASTER IN SNOW, CHRISTMAS IN MUD; CHRISTMAS IN SNOW, EASTER IN MUD.

## APHIDS

Aphids are soft-bodied plant lice and their only redeeming feature is that they are easy to see. They attack nearly all plants, puncturing stem tips and new growth to suck the sap, thus deforming the leaves and new tips. Clumps of certain herbs and flowers will help keep your precious plants aphid-free. Both chives and tansy will make the area less attractive to them. Nasturtiums, especially red and yellow ones, should also be planted around areas you wish to protect. Ladybirds are the aphid's natural enemy. Just one can eat up to 400 in a week or so, so if you see a ladybird, never adjure it to 'fly away home'.

An old wives' tale which is worth a try is to blind the little beasts. Seriously, placing sheets of shiny aluminium foil around the base of a plant, to catch and reflect the sun's rays, is thought to repel aphids. Similarly, twisting narrow spirals of foil around the roots of young cabbage plants is said to inhibit the larvae of the greedy cabbage fly.

*See also Cabbages; Caterpillars; Ladybird; Nasturtiums; O For An Onion; Parsley; Romantic Rose; Zucchini*

## APPLES OF YOUR EYE

The apple has symbolised fruitfulness and been used to divine the future since the days of medieval England. Lancelot was sleeping under an enchanted apple tree when the four fairy queens spirited him away, and Arthur's last resting place was said to have been Avalon, or the Isle of Apples. The last apple of the year's crop should be left for the gnarled old elf known as the Apple Tree Man, to ensure a good harvest the coming year.

Apple growers say they would rather gather their apples under a shrinking moon, for even if the apples are bruised in the gathering they will not rot so fast as if they had been taken at the waxing moon:

*If apples bloom in March*
*In vain for them you'll search.*
*If apples bloom in April*
*Why, then they'll be plentiful.*
*If apples bloom in May*
*You'll eat them night and day.*

Apples are known to have been collected as food by prehistoric man. Writers in the early *Herballs* emphasised the need for care when harvesting and cultivating apples. Thomas Tusser, in his *Five Hundred Pointes of Good Husbandrie* (1580) wrote:

> *Forget it not*
> *Fruit bruised will rot.*
> *Light ladder and long*
> *Doth the tree least wrong.*

Apple cookery, apple confectionery and the production of cider were all very important to early farming communities, so it is not surprising that much ceremony attended the apple harvest. The custom of 'wassailing the apple trees' is still practised in some parts of England. In this ceremony, the farmer and his family visit the orchard, placing offerings of cider and roasted apples in the branches of those trees which have borne well in the year. They then make the following toast:

> *Here's to thee, old apple tree!*
> *When thou may'st bud and*
> *whence thou may'st grow,*
> *Hats full! Caps full! Bushel,*
> *bushel-bags full!*
> *And my pockets full, too! Huzzah!*

They would then fire off guns and all the women and men would shout and sing. The apple trees with poor yields were not so honoured.

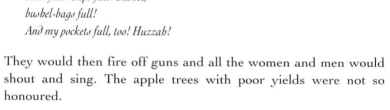

## Apple-Mint Relish

*450 g (15 oz) cooking apples, peeled, cored and
chopped*
*2 onions*
*½ cup chopped mint*
*1⅔ cups (400 ml/13½ fl oz) vinegar*
*170 g (5½ oz) brown sugar*
*1 dried red chili*
*½ cup (85 g/3 oz) raisins*
*1 teaspoon black peppercorns, crushed*
*½ teaspoon coriander seeds*
*1 teaspoon salt*

Place the apples in a pan with the onions,
mint, vinegar, salt, sugar and raisins.
Bring it slowly to boiling point. Place the
chili, peppercorns and coriander seeds in
a muslin spice bag and add to the
mixture. Simmer for about 1½ hours,
uncovered, stirring occasionally, until
thickened. Remove the spice bag and
spoon the relish into warmed, sterilised
jars. Cover, then seal with non-metallic
lids.

*See also Chives; Potatoes*

## THE ANCIENT ASH

The ash tree has an important place in any
garden and has been associated with spells and
divination in much the same way as the oak. Its
magical reputation stems from the ancient writings of
Norse holy men. They believed that the first man on earth was
named Askr, because he was created from the wood of an ash tree.
Druids' wands were made from ash twigs and, moreover, the ash
has healing properties. In early homoeopathic practice, weak-
limbed children were passed through a split ash tree which was
then bound up. If the tree grew again soundly, so would the child.

## ASHES

In Germany, fragments of the charred Yule log would be scattered around fruit trees in an orchard. Flattered, the trees would thus be encouraged to produce a good crop for the next harvest season.

*See also Snails*

## ASPARAGUS

Asparagus and tomatoes are mutual friends and grow well together. Solanine, an enzyme found in the tomato fruit, is a specific antagonist of the vicious asparagus beetle. Parsley and basil planted near asparagus will give added vigour to all three.

*See also Nematodes; Parsley; Skin Care*

IF THE GRASS BE DRY AT MORNING LIGHT,
LOOK FOR RAIN BEFORE THE NIGHT.

## ASTERS

Purple asters drive away snakes, while nettles protect a house from lightning. Rich red peonies are said to glow at night and frighten any lurking spirit. The Chinese call them 'King of the Flowers' and believe they will bring long life to a family, with the bonus of protecting them against insanity.

Asters will also indicate the state of the soil. The purple-stemmed variety (*Aster puniceus*) denotes a need for drainage, while the sea aster (*Aster tripolium*) grows near the sea and collects salt in its tissues. Pests find the leaves bitter and disagreeable, so they make a good massed display near a doorway or greenhouse.

*See also Insect Repellents*

## ASTRAL DAZE

American Ozark farmers, who plant and harvest according to zodiacal lore, advise that flowers and shrubs be planted and propagated during Virgo's ascendant. Often depicted carrying a posy of blossoms, she is said to encourage the growth of all flowers.

Lavender is deemed to be under the dominion of wing-footed Mercury, the fastest of the planets, which rules the witty and versatile Gemini and the modest, diligent Virgo. Nonetheless, it is said to be a plant of peace. Astrally-inclined gardeners held that ' ... the floures would dooble if planted when Mercury was aligned with the Sunne.'

WASH YOUR FACE IN DEW ON THE FIRST DAY IN MAY AND YOU WILL HAVE A GOOD COMPLEXION.

## BASIL

Most of the basils are repellent to all insects except bees. Tomatoes, especially, are not only delighted with basil as a culinary partner but they seem to be protected by it in the vegetable garden. Tomatoes seem to be fuller-flavoured and more aromatic when basil has been grown with them. Fruit flies dislike basil, as do aphids, white flies and those all-too-common houseflies. A bunch of basil hanging over open windows and doors in summer is a refreshingly aromatic and effective fly deterrent.

Despite a vexed reputation amongst the English (early herbalists were convinced that scorpions bred in its roots!) basil has long been a popular culinary herb. Basil has a special affinity with tomatoes and other summer vegetables. The Italians also add it to fish soups and pound it with pine nuts, Parmesan cheese and garlic to make their famous *pesto* sauce. To preserve the flavour of basil year-round, steep the aromatic leaves in a bottle of good quality white wine vinegar.

## BATH SACHETS

Special herbs soothe and hydrate skin exposed to impure air and harsh water. Wrap herbs in pretty cambric or cheesecloth and either toss the little bundle into the water with you, or tie it to the water tap and let the water pulse through the herbs. Save used herbs and use them first as a body scrub and then as a mulch for your plants. Soak in your herbal bath for at least 20 minutes with one of these recipes.

**Rejuvenating Bath** *1 tablespoon each lavender, rosemary, peppermint, lemon balm and comfrey leaf.*

**Hydrating Bath** *1 tablespoon each chamomile, orange flowers, grated orange peel, rose buds and rose hips.*

**Fragrant Bath** *1 tablespoon each chamomile, rosemary, sage, rose hips, acacia, rose petals, sandalwood and honeysuckle flowers.*

Mix the herbs well and spray with a bit of your favourite essential oil for extra fragrance. Place the mixture in an airtight jar or fill a small basket with individual bath bags, tied with narrow satin ribbons.

   *See also Asparagus; Bee-youtiful Plants; Fruit Growing; Hanging Baskets*

## BATTERED BLOSSOMS

The half-opened flowers and buds of pumpkins or squash are a real taste treat. Trim the stalks, wipe them with a moistened paper towel to clean them and allow them to air-dry thoroughly. Then dip them in a thin batter and fry them in a light olive oil, allowing them to drain on absorbent paper, so they are light and crisp. Serve them with garlic salt or sea salt and freshly-ground black pepper.

## BAY LEAVES

Grubs and caterpillars give the pungently aromatic foliage of the bay tree a wide berth, so set more susceptible plants nearby for added protection. Placing dried bay leaves in jars of stored grain, such as oats, rice or beans, will effectively discourage weevils.

Scattering the leaves on pantry shelves will help keep ants at bay. They may even be folded with winter woollies, as a substitute for poisonous moth balls, if you are concerned about curious toddlers meddling in drawers. (Speaking of mothballs, they don't just work against moths. A handful of crushed mothballs mixed through the soil where you are planting carrots will repel the greedy carrot fly larvae.)

Early physicians and *herbwyfes* used oil of bay to relieve arterial conditions. Gypsies, when travelling near the sea, would souse herrings in vinegar and put a bay leaf in each, before baking them over a slow fire. This is an excellent recipe for anyone with a heart condition who is trying to adhere to a healthy diet, because fish—especially oily fish like herring and mackerel—are indicated for cardiovascular conditions.

*See also Moth Deterrents*

## BEANS

French or dwarf beans stay healthy and happy when planted with beetroot, potatoes or strawberry plants. Omnivorous plants, they thrive if composted with hair clippings, sodden newspaper strips or pet hair combings. Fed on such a mineral-rich diet, beans have the ability to fix nitrogen in the soil and therefore help the growth of plants which follow after them. Beans also do well when planted next to cucumbers or carrots but they will grow sharply away from any members of the onion family.

Corn and beans make excellent companions. Not only are the corn rows useful windbreaks for the beans, but the beans can climb up the cornstalks. At the same time the beans' thick foliage around the base of the corn stalk helps deter vermin from scrabbling up and gnawing on the corn kernels.

*See also Cabbage; Potatoes; Strawberries*

## BEE-YOUTIFUL PLANTS

A garden favoured by bees was once thought to be truly blessed because bees, with their ability to make both honey and wax for votive candles, were considered the 'little winged messengers of God'.

Encourage these diligent little plant-pollinators to come to your garden by planting the scented herbs which they love. Lemon balm rubbed on a hive will keep bees together and, if they stray, bees will home to the scent of balm. Basil, dill, lavender, meadowsweet and the summer and winter savories are all adored by bees, as is the pink- or blue-flowered hyssop, first mentioned in the Bible as one of the 'bitter' herbs. When planning a vegetable garden, plant lemon balm or another of these herbs nearby, so bees are attracted to the area, thus ensuring good crop pollination. Similarly, bee-attracting plants should be planted in orchards, to avoid poor fruit-set or failure to fruit, especially on avocado, apricot or citrus trees.

*See also Hyssop; Mint Source*

## BEE STINGS

Old herbalists recommended rubbing bee and wasp stings with mint leaves. Nicolas Culpeper specifically recommended a poultice of mashed rose petals and mint leaves to draw out an embedded sting. A sprig of either of the savories rubbed on a bee sting also gives relief, while marigold flowers were once believed to reduce the pain of a sting from a wasp. (Interestingly, many herbalists today will still use a cooling infusion of marigold petals to treat rashes or recurring sores, to promote healing and relieve infected insect bites, thus reducing scarring.)

Here's another tip to save yourself (and the bee) next time you bump into each other in the garden.

The best way to remove a bee resting on, say, your arm, is to blow it. Bees are susceptible to wind and, more often than not, if you blow on them they'll fly away. If you *do* get stung, don't try to pull the stinger out. Take a knife blade or a (clean!) fingernail and scrape the stinger sideways. That will remove the poison. The stinger is a pulsing muscle that continues to pump, even after it is out of the bee. So, once the poison is removed from it, it will continue to pump, eventually working itself out of the skin.

By the way, avoid eating anything sweet, especially sugary fruit like bananas, before or during your time in the garden. All insects love sweet things and bees are more likely to be attracted to the odour of your skin and hands after a sugary snack. If you must nibble, snack on something savoury—cheese, pickles or a garlicky dip.

*See also Mint Source*

## BERGAMOT

As well as being an attractive garden plant, an infusion of dried bergamot leaves makes a delightful scented tea. In fact, the famous Earl Grey tea is flavoured with oil of bergamot. The refreshing orangey flavour will enhance salads, cream cheese, dips or summer drinks. It also combines well with different meat dishes, notably pork and veal.

WHEN THE RING AROUND THE MOON IS FAR—RAIN IS SOON;
WHEN THE RING AROUND THE MOON IS NEAR—RAIN IS FAR.

A FOOT OF RAIN
WILL KILL HAY AND GRAIN.

## BIRDS

Birds around the garden are among the best insect and pest controllers you can have. To attract birds to your garden, set up feeders and a bird bath or pool. Birds love sunflowers and honeysuckle. Evergreens and thorny plants also attract them as potential nesting sites. Unfortunately, these feathered friends will also seek out any fruiting plants or berry canes, much to the chagrin of the grower! If the birds are a problem, they may be deterred with time-honoured methods like tying tin cans or bright ribbons to tree branches, or criss-crossing a plant with white thread, tinsel or fishing line, so they do not feel confident about being able to land. A Chinese idea is to hang large slices of onion in fruit trees. Apparently, birds dislike the smell.

*See also Mulberries; Strawberries*

## BODY OIL

Is your garden overflowing with fragrant blossoms? Capture these scents by creating your own perfumed oils. Fill a jar with fresh flowers like honeysuckle, rose and jasmine. Cover them with pure coconut oil and leave in a warm spot for at least 48 hours. Strain out the flowers and keep the oil in a cool, dark place. It may be used as a perfume, a scented body oil or a delightful massage oil.

WHEN BEANS ARE IN FLOWER, FOOLS ARE IN FLOWER.

13

IF MORNING GLORIES GROW IN YOUR GARDEN EVEN THOUGH YOU
HAVE NOT PLANTED THEM, IT IS A SIGN YOU ARE MUCH LOVED.

## BODY POWDERS

Body powders are cooling, smooth and
fragrant—a delightful finale to a relaxing
bath. Loosely fill a china jar with
the bruised petals of fragrant
flowers, picked at the height of
their scent. Gardenia, jasmine and
rose petals all have a strong scent
which is distinctive, yet delicate. Top
up the jar with a mixture of 5 parts
cornstarch to 1 part arrowroot, plus 1
teaspoon of rice. (This helps keep the
powder dry.) After 2 weeks, sift the powder
into a jar with a secure lid and add a pretty
powder puff. An excellent cooling and
absorbent baby powder is made by combining
2 parts arrowroot, 1 part chamomile flowers
and 1 part marigold flowers, then grinding them
all to a fine powder.

IN GERMANY, KNOTS IN OAK TREES ARE SAID TO BE FAIRY DOORS.

## BOOKMARKS

Many years ago, costmary was known as the 'Bible leaf' because
of the custom of using it as a fragrant bookmark in Bibles and
prayer books. Costmary, or any other large, scented leaves, such
as those of the rose geranium, lemon verbena, tansy, borage or
eucalyptus, still make charming bookmarks. If, like women of
olden days, you want to enjoy them chiefly for their fragrance,
then press and mount them on cards. However, done this way, the
herbs will soon crumble. If you're making the bookmarks as gifts,
it is better to press them between pieces of blotting paper or tissue
in the pages of one or two heavy books. Then, when the leaves are
dry, place them between two sheets of stiff, transparent plastic

film, cut to the size and shape you wish. (Acetate sheets for making overhead transparencies, or stiff plastic packaging, will do nicely.) Either seal with glue or punch holes around the edges and lace them together with pretty yarn or embroidery silk.

## BORAGE

Louis XIV took a pretty straightforward approach when planting borage in his gardens at Versailles. He simply wanted to enjoy the beauty of its vivid blue flowers. The ancient Roman naturalist, Pliny, looked deeper than this, maintaining that this herb brought courage to a home's inhabitants and saved those within from 'melancholy'. Savory, more prosaically, would keep fleas and vermin at bay. Borage, 'the herb of gladness', has long been used as a medicine for circulatory disorders and gypsy women used compresses of borage to ward off varicose veins.

*See also Bookmarks; Vinegars*

## BRUISES

Potatoes are the richest natural source of potassium chloride and raw potatoes can be very useful in a gardener's first aid kit. Use a raw, peeled, grated potato in a poultice around a sprain of any kind. Hot, baked potato pulp can also be applied to relieve gardener's elbow or other joint pain. A potato poultice is also a remarkable remedy for bruises. However, if your vegetable drawer yields only a cabbage, break the ridges of the larger outer leaves, dip them into boiling water and apply them to the bruise to reduce swelling. The cheerful common daisy was once called 'bruisewort'. To reduce swelling, crush the leaves and flowers and add them to wheatgerm oil or infuse them in water and rub the oil or infusion gently into the bruise. Lavender and rosemary infusions will also help relieve a bruise.

IF BEANS GROW UPSIDE-DOWN IN THEIR PODS,

IT IS A SIGN OF A YEAR OF PLENTY.

## BUTTERFLY PLANTS

Attract these living jewels to your garden by planting the flowers and shrubs that they love best. Butterflies are often observed in the vicinity of lavender, marigolds, honeysuckles and chrysanthemums—all the plants used to enhance the traditional, cottage-style garden. Most of the favoured 'butterfly plants' have strong, sweet scents and bright colours. Even brightly-coloured stones and pebbles will attract their interest. The most potent effect is gained with buddleia, the aptly-named 'butterfly bush'. A piece of old Welsh lore refers to the quaint practice of 'calling the butterflies', whereby the housewife would stand at the back door and wave an armful of buddleia in full flower. Shortly she would be surrounded by fluttering clouds of ecstatic tortoiseshell butterflies.

Other plants which butterflies particularly like include clover, forget-me-nots, cornflowers and thyme. Lobelia is also said to be much favoured by butterflies, while Michaelmas daisies encourage them to stay in your garden through the dying days of autumn. Several Australian native wildflowers, notably grevilleas, are butterfly specialists, too. Along with wattle, plumbago and wild passionfruit, these should attract clouds of gentle and pretty butterflies.

Enchanted by these colourful gems and hoping one will alight on your head or finger for luck? Try reciting the following Yorkshire charm. Stand with eyes closed and hands outstretched and say, 'La, la, let; my bonnie, bonnie pet'.

IF THE DOWN FLIES OFF DANDELIONS OR THISTLES WHEN THERE IS NO WIND, IT IS A SIGN OF RAIN.

RED SKY IN THE MORNING, SHEPHERD'S WARNING;
RED SKY AT NIGHT, SHEPHERD'S DELIGHT.

## CABBAGES

Cabbages dislike strawberries and tomatoes but, like all members of the *Brassicacae* family, are greatly helped by aromatic herbs such as rosemary and sage, which repel the voracious cabbage white butterfly. Plant orange nasturtiums amongst your cabbages to deter aphid attack. In England, the national research station for organic gardening endorses alternating French beans with cabbages to provide natural, non-chemical protection against cabbage root fly. The shape of the beans confuses the vision or 'radar' of the cabbage root fly, which is conditioned to home in on anything cabbage-shaped, and thus forces it to move off.

*See also Aphids; Chamomile; Lavender; Potatoes; Strawberries*

## CARAWAY CHARM

Caraway has long been regarded as a protective and binding herb and was credited with the power to prevent witchcraft and theft. Caraway seeds were mixed with pigeons' and hens' feed to make them return to their coops. Noting this, wives insured against the advances of other women by slipping a few caraway seeds into their husbands' pockets and, as recently as World War I, soldiers' sweethearts gave them caraway-seed-based buns to bind their affections while away.

## CARROTS

There is no question about the better results when carrots are planted with onions, shallots, leeks or peas. Carrot-fly maggots, which attack the roots of the plants, don't like pungent smells, so plant wormwood or sage nearby for additional protection. In the pantry, store carrots well away from apples, or they will become bitter-tasting.

*See also Beans; Lavender; Lettuce; O For An Onion; Parsley*

## CARTWHEEL GARDENS

An old-fashioned way to enjoy aromatic plants is to set them in a circle, about 2–2½ m (6½–8 ft) in diameter, with rows from the centre to the edges. This idea came from the custom of using abandoned cartwheels as planters in cottage gardens.

A charming variation is to use different varieties of the same herb in the alternating spokes of the wheel—for instance, green then gold marjoram; or golden thyme (*Thymus vulgaris* 'Aureum'), then its pink-stemmed cousin. Plant the 'wheel' where the sun shines directly upon it, to maximise its impact on the eye and its fragrance.

# CATERPILLARS

White pepper sprinkled on vegetables will repel caterpillars, as will a chili 'tea' spray, made by blending a few finely-chopped chilies with water and pure soap flakes. A garlic spray will control most garden pests and is very easy to make:

Soak 6 to 8 cloves of garlic in a cupful of kerosene for 48 hours. Dissolve 10 g (⅓ oz) of soap flakes in hot water, top up with enough water to make 500 ml (16 fl oz) and add to the garlic mixture. Strain and store in a labelled, tightly-sealed jar. Dilute 1 part garlic mixture to 5 of water when making up the spray — dilute it more for delicate plants like ferns.

Wormwood 'tea' spray will control whitefly, aphids and tomato fly. Cover 2 or 3 handfuls of chopped leaves with boiling water and leave to stand for 3 hours. Mix 1 part of this solution with 4 parts of water.

A rather gruesome but undeniably satisfying treatment for marauding caterpillars is 'bug juice', made by squishing as many caterpillars as possible, putting the bodies in a covered bucket and letting them stew in the sun with a bit of water for a few weeks. The resultant sludge makes absolutely terrific plant food, with the bonus of giving any fresh battalions of caterpillars a mighty fright ...

*See also Bay Leaves; Pepper*

SHE WALKS AMONG THE LOVELINESS SHE MADE,
BETWEEN THE APPLE BLOSSOMS AND THE WATER—
SHE WALKS AMONG THE PATTERNED PIED BROCADE,
EACH FLOWER HER SON AND EVERY TREE HER DAUGHTER.

VITA SACKVILLE-WEST (1926)

## CATNIP

The pretty catnip or catmint is thought to be irresistible to cats, according to this old saying:

*If you set it, the cats will eat it;*
*If you sow it, the cats don't know it.*

Even if you don't have a moggy, there are many reasons to plant this herb in your garden. Rats and mice are repelled by it and since ancient times it has been planted around crops to disperse these vermin. Similarly, freshly-picked catnip may be placed on the barbecue table to keep ants at bay and the powdered dried leaves may be rubbed into your pet's coat to repel fleas.

## CHAMOMILE

The pretty feathery-leaved chamomile is known as the 'plant doctor', being a friend to most things growing in the garden. Mint becomes tastier if chamomile is near and ailing flowers revive. A cupful of chamomile tea, made from soaking the flowers overnight, will often bring round a sickly house plant. Cabbages enjoy having chamomile around their skirts, as do lettuces.
   *See also Cuts And Grazes;*
*Lavender; O For An Onion; Paths*

## CHAMOMILE LAWN

Chamomile was used in Tudor times to make aromatic lawns. It is likely that Sir Francis Drake played his famous game of bowls upon a chamomile lawn, for grass ones were actually quite rare then. It may seem surprising, but the first grass lawns, as we know them, were not sown until the 18th century.

To make an aromatic chamomile lawn, sow seed in early spring. First mark an area for the lawn, then scatter seed sparingly—a handful produces more than 1000 plants. Rake in the seed and water it gently. When plants first show, keep the soil moist and thin the plants to about 15 cm (6 in) apart, moving excess seedlings to bald patches. Keeping the area free from weeds during the first year will see the chamomile spread, suppressing all weeds from then onwards. Mowing once every few months will encourage the plants to thicken up, and by the second year, you will be able to enjoy the fruity perfume as you stroll about your chamomile lawn.

## CHAPPED HANDS

Chapped hands are sore and inconvenient. Investigate your kitchen cupboards for fast-acting, easy-to-prepare remedies. For instance, leftover cooked, mashed potatoes, mixed with a little almond oil and orange flower water, make a soothing and effective hand treatment. For severe chapping, or plant allergy-induced eczema, Maurice Messegue's recipe for hand 'bath' works as well today as it did in the 18th century and is a positive (and cheaper) alternative to topical cortisone-based treatments. Steep equal parts of artichoke leaves, lavender flowers and diced chicory root in hot water for 10 to 15 minutes, then strain. Dip your hands into the warm infusion for 5 minutes at a time.

Apple cider vinegar is an inexpensive and effective old-style remedy for chapped hands or dry, flaky skin. Massage it into clean hands and let it dry, then apply a light hand lotion. Your skin will stay soft and supple, even after hours of work in the garden. An Epsom salts soak also works wonders on sore or scratched hands.

The best cure for chapped hands, as with all hand problems, is

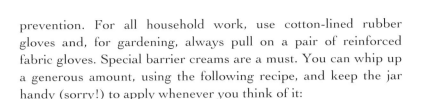

prevention. For all household work, use cotton-lined rubber gloves and, for gardening, always pull on a pair of reinforced fabric gloves. Special barrier creams are a must. You can whip up a generous amount, using the following recipe, and keep the jar handy (sorry!) to apply whenever you think of it:

## Barrier Cream

*30 g (1 oz) lanolin*
*30 g (1 oz) beeswax*
*90 ml (3 fl oz) almond oil*
*90 ml (3 fl oz) your favourite floral or herbal infusion*
*pinch of borax*
(Handle the borax with care as it is toxic in neat form. In the recipe, the small amount spread through the ingredients is not a problem, once it is made up.)

Melt and blend all ingredients together over a slow flame, stirring constantly. Pot up when the mixture thickens and has cooled slightly.

# CHERVIL

Chervil is a pretty herb with feathery leaves. It was much used in medieval times in soups and 'sallets' and in France today the parboiled roots, fried in butter, are regarded as a delicacy. The leaves may be chopped finely and used as a garnish or to season cheese or potato dishes. It also goes well with fish, eggs, chicken or veal and enhances many vegetables, especially carrots. Try adding chopped chervil to scrambled eggs or omelettes, or use it in quiche fillings.

The leaves of chervil are blood-cleansing and diuretic, a boon to people suffering from rheumatism. Gypsies would take an infusion of chervil if they had a fever. By increasing perspiration, the temperature was lowered.

*See also Radishes*

## CHICKENS

Poultry farmers and other bird keepers find it useful to grow mustard around birds' cages or chicken runs, because it seems to repel bird lice and also disinfect the soil. Nettles are another useful fodder plant and tonic for animals, especially poultry. Chopped nettles added to baby chicks' feed makes them more resistant to coccidiosis and diarrhoea.

## CHILD'S PLAY

Never forget the simple pleasures of a garden from a child's point of view. Not everything need be pickled or preserved for domestic use. For instance, when pruning your fuchsia, be sure to make a few 'ballerinas' for a small child by tweaking off the appropriate outer petals and stamens.

Birds and bees sip nectar from flowers and children can, too. Just nip off the end of the little tube of a honeysuckle and let them sip the honey out of it. You can do the same thing with the bright red blossoms of a salvia plant.

Hold golden dandelion blossom under a child's chin and ask, 'Will you be wealthy when you grow up?' If there is a yellow glow on his or her chin, the answer is yes. You can also teach children to find out if their friends like butter by using buttercups in the same way. Blow out the seeds of the dandelion head to see if a child's mother wants the child to go home, or to tell what time it is. The number of seeds left after blowing three times will tell the time.

Of course, daisies and clover can be made into chains or plaited into crowns. Start plaiting with three stems of unequal lengths. When you come to the end of the shortest stem, add another daisy and keep plaiting. Children also love to play the 'daisy game'. Pluck one petal at a time, saying, 'He (or she!) loves me, loves me not'. If the answer is 'not', then try another daisy!

## CHILIES

Chilies are a favourite for flavouring fruit and vegetable chutneys. Long used by herbalists as a digestive and to combat colds and 'flu, hot chilies are increasingly used now, with the popularity of Cajun and Eastern cuisines. Be careful when preparing the chilies, as they can burn the skin fiercely. Avoid touching your face or eyes unless you have washed your hands *thoroughly*.

### Lime-Chili Pickles

*6 limes*
*1 tablespoon whole black peppercorns*
*1 tablespoon cumin*
*3 red chilies, peeled, seeded and minced*
*2 garlic cloves, crushed*
*1 tablespoon mustard seeds*
*1 bay leaf*
*300 ml (10 fl oz) olive oil*

Cut the limes into wedges and combine them with the peppercorns, cumin and chilies in an enamel or stainless steel saucepan, over a very low heat. Add the remaining ingredients, except for the oil, and fill warmed, sterile jars with the mixture. Pour sufficient olive oil into each jar to cover the contents. Make temporary lids of absorbent paper, and secure them with an elastic band around the neck of each jar. Leave the jars on a sunny windowsill for 6 days, then seal them firmly with airtight lids and store. After 2 or 3 weeks, the lime rinds will have softened and absorbed the flavours of the aromatic oil and spicy chilies. Use them as a garnish for fish or chicken, add them to salads with mint sprigs, to a dish of natural yoghurt, or use them as an accompaniment to curries.

IF YOU MAKE A CROWN OF BLACKTHORN TWIGS, THEN BAKE IT UNTIL IT HAS TURNED TO ASH, AND SCATTER THIS ASH ON PLANTS BEFORE DAWN ON NEW YEAR'S MORNING, YOU CAN BE SURE OF GOOD CROPS.

## CHIVES

Chives have an excellent reputation for helping neighbouring plants in the garden. Parsley seems to grow bigger, greener and lusher when inter-planted with chives. Chives were often used by farmers of old to keep their apple trees free from scab.
*See also Aphids*

## CHOKOS

An economic and plentiful plant, chokos—also known as the Mexican *chayote*—are a familiar sight in many a temperate garden, trailing over fences and outhouses. They are sociable plants and seem to grow best in tandem. Plant two vines together to ensure abundant fruiting. Chokos may be prepared in a variety of ways, which, due to their formidable capacity to reproduce, is indeed fortunate. Try them as a vegetable side dish with a creamy cheese sauce, or as a substitute for apples in pies or strudel. Alternatively, try this deliciously simple soup recipe:

### Choko Soup

*3 large chokos, peeled and chopped*
*2 leeks, peeled and sliced*
*3 cups (750 ml/24 fl oz) chicken stock*
*½ cup (125 ml/4 fl oz) cream*
*freshly ground black pepper*
*sea or rock salt*
*extra cream, snipped chives and a dash of paprika, to garnish*

Place the chokos, leeks and stock in a saucepan, bring to the boil, then reduce the heat. Simmer for 15 to 20 minutes. Mash and sieve them, or blend them in a food processor until smooth. Stir the cream through and season with black pepper and salt to taste. Garnish and serve.

To grow large cabbages, let an old woman plant the seed, sitting on the ground, then walk away without looking backwards.

## CHRISTMAS CUSTOMS

Christmas brings with it a number of odd superstitions to do with plants and crops. This is especially so in the northern hemisphere, where such customs derived originally from winter solstice rituals. These were celebrated in the dead of winter, hoping to assure a good harvest in the year ahead. For instance:

- a fruit tree could be made to bear by tying a band of straw around its trunk or beating it with a horsewhip on Christmas Day.
- if the sun shone through the fruit trees at noon on Christmas Day, there would be good crops.
- the number of days between the first snowfall and Christmas told how many snowfalls would come before spring.

## CITRUS TREES

An old wives' tale has it that a few zinc-coated nails should be hammered into the trunk of an orange, lime, lemon or grapefruit tree to encourage good cropping. I think this may have had its origins in farming lore, where poor-fruiting trees were 'punished', rather than because of any beneficial effect from the leached metal. However, if you are desperate, try it. It might just work and, either way, you'll feel less frustrated.

*See also Bee-youtiful Plants; Cumquats; Lemony Loveliness*

THE CHAMOMILE SHALL TEACH
THEE PATIENCE,
THAT RISES BEST WHEN WALKED UPON.

## CLEMATIS

In his *Herball*, John Gerard called clematis 'the virgin's bower', indicating that it was once a popular choice for protecting young maidens from both sunshine and the stares of inquisitive passers-by. *Clematis vitalba*, blooming from late summer through to early autumn, is a lovely choice for a bower. Its clusters of greenish-white flowers are followed by masses of feathery seed pods, giving it a misty-grey appearance. These seed heads last into winter, explaining its nickname of 'Old Man's Beard'.

*Clematis flammula*, a native of southern Europe, is also known as 'fragrant bower'. It is just as glorious in an autumn garden, bearing great heads of sweetly-scented, creamy-white flowers. These flowers are followed by fluffy silver seed heads which stay through much of the winter. The clematis takes its name from the Greek *klema*, meaning a 'vine-branch' because, like a grapevine, it climbs only by twisting its tendrils around a support. They like to climb in company with other plants that give shelter to their roots. Clematis prefer a little lime in their soil. Plant them from pots in late spring and cut them back fairly hard at the end of winter. They will grow about 3 m (10 ft) each year.

## CLOVER

The ubiquitous clover is also a happy sign in the garden, according to ancient legend. Beloved of fairies and bees, it bestows the gift of second sight and, of course, there is always the chance of finding a four-leafed one. By the way, a four-leafed clover will break an evil spell.

*See also Butterfly Plants; Child's Play*

## COMPANION PLANTING

Certain plants have a distinct effect on the soil. Their presence as a positive or negative companion for other, subsequent, plants, may be felt long after the original plant has died. For instance, if a fruit tree dies, should it be replaced with another of its own kind? Never. A young apple tree planted on the site of an old one will usually wither and die, because the secretions from the leaves dropped on the soil by its predecessor will poison it. A young cherry planted in the same spot will, on the other hand, thrive.

Similarly, old herbalists advised long ago that a 'hot' herb should always be replaced with a 'cooling' one. In other words, never plant the same one twice in succession. Both of these old wives' tales are based on the sound, commonsense methods of older-style crop rotation, which ensured that the soil did not become exhausted or deficient in particular nutrients over time.

*See also Asparagus; Basil; Beans; Cabbages; Carrots; Chamomile; Chives; Fennel; Fruit Growing; Horseradish; Hyssop; Lavender; Lettuce; Marigold; Marrows; Mulberries; Nettles; O For An Onion; Parsley; Potatoes; Radishes; Romantic Roses; Strawberries; Tansy; Zucchini*

## COWSLIPS

Bavarian farmers have a pretty notion that elves are very fond of cowslips. In order that the elves remain good-humoured and bless the farmers' cattle with sweet frothy milk, the farmers are careful to tie a bunch of these flowers between each cow's horns.

Cowslips are also loved and guarded by fairies; witness Ariel's claim in Shakespeare's *The Tempest:*

> *Where the bee sucks, there suck I,*
> *In a cowslip's bell I lie ...*

Cowslips are thought to have the power to find hidden fairy gold, being keys to unlock the way to treasure. Never pick just one, particularly if they are for a gift.

## CUCUMBERS

Cucumbers are not the easiest of vegetables to grow, being extremely vulnerable to mildew and fungal diseases and especially favoured by nematodes (eelworms). Another problem which can affect cucumber's cropping potential is poor pollination—they do not attract bees by themselves, relying instead on having bee balm or another bee-attracting plant nearby. An ingenious old wives' tale calls for a sugar spray to be used on the cucumbers. Odd as this may sound, it is doubly effective. The sugar has a drying effect on the nematodes (rather like putting salt on snails) and the sweet smell attracts bees.

*See also Beans; Lettuce; Pimples; Potatoes; Radishes*

## CUMQUATS

A quota of cumquats ... Cumquat trees are very pretty but what does one do with a more than generous harvest?

**Cumquats in Syrup**
Prick the fruit all over with a sharp needle, place them in a saucepan and cover them with water. Bring them to the boil and cook gently until the fruit softens slightly. In a separate saucepan, make a syrup from 500 g (16 oz) sugar to 300 ml (10 fl oz) water for every 12 cumquats. Boil this syrup rapidly for 15 minutes. Drain the cumquats and add them to the syrup, reduce the heat and cook for a few minutes more, stirring thoroughly. Spoon the cumquats and syrup into warmed, sterilised jars. Cap securely and label.

## CUT FLOWERS

My mother offers the following six-point plan for making cut flowers last longer:

- Always pick flowers in the cool of the morning or evening, never when the sun is directly overhead.
- Always cut the stems under running water and on an angle.
- Remove all leaves below the water line.
- Change water every day and ensure vases are kept very clean.
- Add a pinch of sugar or an aspirin to the water to stop the flowers from drooping too quickly.
- Crush the stems of woody plants, like hydrangeas. Singe the stems of dahlias and ferns and scrape the last 5 cm (2 in) of rose stems.

She adds that hairspray will keep hibiscus from closing at night and that a pinch of salt should be sprinkled in the centre of camellias to stop them turning brown.

*See also Foxgloves*

## CUTS AND GRAZES

Minor cuts and grazes will benefit from a wash with antiseptic herbs like garlic, onion or chamomile. The bruised leaves and flowers or pulped vegetable will provide emergency dressings. A tiny dab of cayenne powder can stop bleeding from a cut. So does plantain. Even city-dwellers can usually find plantain in their gardens or parks. Use an infusion directly on the wound or add to warm water for a long, soothing soak.

Vitamin C is a powerful bactericide that helps prevent infections. It's well worth remembering if you're a rose grower, in particular. Getting pricked and scratched, while working in a manure-rich garden bed, is the name of the game. To use, put a pinch of vitamin C powder in the bottom of a saucer, mix with water to form a paste and dab it directly onto the wound. It may sting slightly, but remember, it promotes rapid healing and, as a bonus for a really nasty cut, will minimise the risk of scarring.

*See also Aloe Vera*

## CUTWORMS

Cutworms are one of the more wasteful and deceitful pests in the garden. They are wasteful because they attack only the stems of young seedlings, thus destroying the whole plant. They are deceitful because they can camouflage

themselves so well, turning from green to cream to grey, depending on their background. Protect each seedling with a collar made by cutting a ring from cardboard or paper-towelling rolls. Another, more fiddly, idea is to stake each seedling snugly against a toothpick, which makes it more difficult for the cutworm to chomp right through. Extremely satisfying is the suffocation method. If you suspect there are cutworms in the soil, wrap the affected area with cling wrap for 3 weeks and let them sweat it out. Also gratifying is to capitalise on the cutworm's sweet tooth (well, gums) and set baits, made from a sticky mess of molasses and sawdust. The cutworms will gorge themselves and, sticky and helpless, will lie on top of the soil till they either die from the heat or are snapped up by birds.

IF IT RAINS WITH THE SEA'S FLOW, THEE CAN GO OUT TO MOW;
IF IT RAINS WITH THE SEA'S EBB, THEE CAN GO BACK TO BED.

## DAFFODILS

Pliny declared that daffodil bulbs scared thieves and 'drove rats from their holes'. Always plant more yellow daffodils than white ones, as this means you will always possess more gold than silver.

## DANDELIONS

The dandelion, which 16th century herbalist Nicolas Culpeper named 'piss-a-bed', is one of the best diuretics in Nature. Gypsies used fresh dandelion leaves in salad and made coffee from the dried roots. They also turned the golden flowers into wonderful wine. Dandelion 'milk' is an old cure for warts. Touch the wart with the juice and leave it to dry. Repeat often, and eventually the wart will drop off.

*See also Child's Play; Fragrance*

## DILL

Dill is usually regarded as an essential herb in a cook's garden, being the chief flavouring ingredient for pickling cucumbers and a tasty addition to salads, dressings and steamed vegetables. Dill leaves are also good with fish, shellfish, creamed or cottage cheese dishes and eggs. Fresh sprigs of dill flavour and help the digestion of cabbage, sauerkraut and onions. It is no accident that dill's name comes from the old Norse word *dilla*, meaning 'to soothe'. Adding dill to cooking water will also overcome that awful smell.

*See also Bee-youtiful Plants*

SPRING HAS COME WHEN YOU CAN STAND ON DAISIES.

## DOGS

I am not a dog-owner but I'm not a dog-hater either. If other people wish to keep a pup, that's fine, but don't let it do its business in my garden. Some countries now have quite stringent rules about puppy poo and fines are imposed on owners who let their dogs foul the footpaths. Anyway, until we achieve that happy state, I shall hop down off my soapbox and pass on this tip from my mother's neighbour-but-one, who got very cross about her yard being the neighbourhood dogs' favoured spot. Fill a half dozen old, plastic drink bottles with water, cap them and place them out the front of your home. I don't know why or how this works (and it doesn't always work, either), but in her case it did appear to spook the dogs and they hurried on—to the next house! Oh, well. (I've noticed that cats won't drink from a water dish placed too near their litter tray either. Maybe there is a similar association?)

*See also Fennel*

## DRAWER PILLOWS

Drawer pillows are lovely gifts for anyone, including yourself. Make them by cutting fine organdy or taffeta rectangular pouches to fit the base of drawers. Stitch them on three sides and fill them sparingly with dried rose petals, lavender, carnation petals or a

mixture of rose geranium leaves and lemon verbena. Costmary with rose geranium leaves is another nice blend. Then, stitch the fourth seam. Placed in each drawer, these padded liners will effectively perfume your clothes as well as the room.

## DYEPOT FROM NATURE

Most plants yield some colour as a dye, and have an affinity with natural fibres. Wool and silk are best as they take colours more evenly than tough, tightly-woven cotton fibres. Parsley and turmeric produce various shades of yellow; tansy and sorrel give a greener hue; pinks and purples come from madder, blended with hollyhock flowers. Many vegetables, such as red cabbage and onions, can also be used for dyes. Herbs which are not commonly grown in the garden can be bought, dried, from a herbalist or a good craft supplier.

### Marigold Wool Bath

Prepare a dye bath by placing 100 g (3½ oz) dried marigold petals or 300 g (10 oz) fresh flower heads in a muslin bag. Put them into a 5 litre (160 fl oz) enamel bucket and cover them with water. Let the mixture stand overnight.

Next day, fill the bucket with water and bring it slowly to the boil over 1 hour. Simmer for a further hour, cool and strain.

Dissolve 25 g (1 oz) alum and 5 g (¼ oz) cream of tartar and pour this mixture through 100 g (3½ oz) of raw wool yarn, which has been thoroughly wetted and tied in a loose hank. Soak the yarn in the dye mixture and bring it slowly to the boil.

When the wool has reached the desired intensity of colour, remove it, squeeze out excess dye and rinse it gently in another bucket of water about the same temperature as the wool, *not* under the running tap. (It is important not to change the water temperature too quickly as this will cause the wool to felt.) Hang it up to dry in a warm, shady place, well away from direct heat or sunlight.

## ELDER

The elder tree is sometimes a witch in disguise and should never be pruned without first asking her permission with this old rhyme:

> *Ould gal, give me some of thy wood*
> *An Oi will give some of moine*
> *When Oi grows inter a tree.*

An old English divination game entails binding green ash twigs together and placing them on the fire to burn. Each twig is named for an unmarried girl in the household. She whose band breaks first will be the first to wed. Should she have children, though, they must never be laid in a cradle made from elder wood, for the elder witch will pinch them black and blue.

*See also Insomnia*

## EXERCISES

It was Charles Warner who grimly observed that 'What a man needs in gardening is a cast-iron back, with a hinge in it'. How right he was! For those of us who tend to rush out seasonally and put in long hours for a short time, these pre-gardening exercises can help ease muscles into action.

For pulling and tugging at weeds, which can strain the shoulders and neck, warm up by clasping your hands behind your waist and stretching your shoulders back, gently lifting your arms as high as possible. Roll your shoulders forward, clasp your hands behind your neck and slowly rock forward. Gently press your head down to stretch your spine.

Next, stand and stretch your under-arm muscles. Slip your left hand behind your back, reach over your right shoulder with your right hand and clasp your hands together behind you. Grip tightly and stretch gently.

Stretch your legs. With your legs spread wide, lean over to grasp your ankles and pull your forehead forward towards them.

For pruning, stand with your feet wide apart and stretch your arms overhead. Throw your arms down through your legs and

swing your body, reaching and stretching your head a little further each time.

For crouching, which can strain your back and thighs, kneel and slowly raise and lower your upper body several times. Keep your back straight and your movements controlled.

IF CHRISTMAS DAY ON THURSDAY BE,
A WINDY WINTER SHALL YE SEE;
WINDY WEATHER IN EACH WEEK
AND HARD TEMPEST, STRONG AND THICK.
THE SUMMER SHALL BE GOOD AND DRY,
CORN AND BEAST SHALL MULTIPLY.

## FAIRY FLORA

The Irish believe lily of the valley is a fairy flower and warn that, since the little people use the stems as ladders, it should be planted in an undisturbed corner of the garden. Be wary of stepping around there, for it's assured a fairy horse will rise under you and spirit you miles away, leaving you lost and exhausted when the dawn breaks. Bluebells are quite safe when planted in a garden, but you should never wander alone in a wood where they grow, for fairies might kidnap you. Pay heed to this slightly sinister tune for a child's skipping game:

*In and out the dusky bluebells,*
*I am your master;*
*Tipper-ipper-apper on your shoulder,*
*I am your master ...*

The Scottish name for bluebells is 'deadman's bells', for to hear the ring of a bluebell is to hear one's own death knell. The bluebell is one of the most potent of all fairy flowers and a bluebell wood at dusk, though enchanting, can be a hazardous place.

The Irish scatter primroses on the front doorstep to encourage good fairies to dance there at night, and hang a cross made from yarrow behind the door as protection against witches. Sweetbriar and honeysuckle over the door also keep evil spirits at bay, while hollyhocks and snapdragons are useful for breaking bad spells.

*See also Cowslips; Pansies; Touch Wood; Witches*

# FENNEL

To sow the bronze, feathery leaves of fennel is said to sow trouble. As with much gardening folklore, this superstition is based on fact, for fennel appears to seriously retard the growth of any nearby plants. A bed of pennyroyal can help to rectify the problem, for it is thought to somehow purify the soil around it.

Fennel is an easy herb to grow and, with its pretty, fringed foliage and large umbels of golden flowers, it is a surprisingly decorative plant to have in a garden. Fennel is a traditional seasoning for fish and, if baking or barbecuing a whole fish, branches of fennel make a fragrant base for it to rest on while cooking. Fennel goes well with difficult-to-digest foods, such as cabbage and onions.

Not surprisingly, in light of this, its seeds were once made into a tea to soothe colicky babies. Try using fennel as an alternative to mint and add the chopped leaves to yoghurt, hummus or other pulse dishes.

If you have a dog, you should plant fennel in your garden, because it will help to repel fleas. However, most plants dislike it, so keep it away from other flower beds. Fennel itself is retarded in the presence of coriander and will not form seeds, while wormwood will kill it off very quickly.

WHEN THE WIND IS IN THE NORTH-WEST,
THERE'LL BE WEATHER AT ITS BEST.

## FERTILISERS

Some of the best fertilisers for your garden have very humble origins. For instance, nutrients needed by plants (such as calcium, sodium, silica, magnesium, phosphorus and potash) are present in generous helpings in the ordinary banana skin. Simply tear the skin into little pieces and tuck them into the topsoil around plants. Banana skins and apple cores are both the special favourites of roses and ferns, while a 'tea' made by stewing eggshells in a bucket of water is the best pick-me-up ever for geraniums.

*See also Milk; Nettles; Poo*

## FEVER

A helpful bedtime drink for a patient suffering from a feverish cold may be made from rosemary and lavender, infused as a tea. A soup made from common sorrel will also help allay distress and fever.

*See also Nervousness*

## FINGERNAILS

To keep fingernails free from dirt, dig them into a cake of soap before you dig into the garden.

## FLORISTS' SECRETS

A secret, closely guarded by ambitious exhibitors in flower shows, capitalises on the 'accelerating' effect of potatoes and apples on other plants. Several weeks before the plant is to be shown, place it in a brown paper bag with potato or apple seedlings for 7–10 days. This should result in a flurry of buds, which will bloom riotously just in time for the judging.

*See also Battered Blossoms; Marigold*

## FLOWERS AS FOOD

Seasoning the main course with herbs is nothing out of the ordinary, but bear in mind that certain flowers can also add a lovely fragrance and a delicate flavour to desserts and some salads. To make a delicious topping for fruit salad, add honeysuckle flowers or rose petals to a cup of double cream, then infuse over a gentle heat for 10–15 minutes (do not boil). Strain. Stir in a teaspoon of sweetened brandy or caster sugar.

### Flowery Pudding

*200 g (7 oz) blueberries or stoned, halved cherries*
*1 handful pink or red rose petals*
*50 g (1½ oz) caster sugar*
*¼ cup (60 ml/2 fl oz) strawberry or pineapple juice*
*8–10 slices of white bread, crusts removed*

Combine the berries and petals. Sprinkle them with sugar, cover and refrigerate overnight. Place the fruit mixture in a non-aluminium saucepan, add the juice and warm slightly. Tear half the slices of bread into quarters and press them around the sides and base of a china pudding bowl to form a lining. Strain the fruit mix, reserving the juice, and pack it into a bowl. Top with the remaining bread slices, pinching around the edges to seal. Drizzle the reserved juices slowly over the top, so they will soak through the bread. Seal the bowl with an inverted plate and refrigerate overnight. Carefully run a wet knife-point around the edge of the dish before turning the pudding out onto a chilled plate. Serve with cream or yoghurt.

A THICK FOG AND SMALL MOON
BRING AN EASTERLY WIND SOON.

IT WILL RAIN IF PIGS APPEAR UNEASY AND ROLL IN THE DUST.

## FOOT CARE

My sworn remedy for reviving feet which are worn out and swollen after a long day in the garden (or anywhere, for that matter), is the old-fashioned foot bath. The herbs to use in a foot bath are any of the stimulant types, such as rosemary, lavender, the mints, yarrow and thyme. Make an infusion of 60 g (2 oz) fresh herbs to 500 ml (17 fl oz) water and add this to a flattish tray of hot water. Try any of the following mixtures for a sublime 'feet treat':

- Combine pine oil, almond oil and a tablespoon of rosemary leaves. Steep them in boiling water and then chill, as a refreshing antidote for tired feet.
- Rub your feet with lemon juice, then take this lavender foot bath to leave your feet feeling soft and fresh. Place one tablespoon each of lavender, sage and thyme, with a teaspoon of salt, in a large bowl. Fill the bowl with boiling water, strain and then add the fluid to warm water. A plunge in cold water afterwards can also help to revive tired feet.
- The old-fashioned mustard bath brings cold, clammy feet back to life. Blend 3 tablespoons of mustard powder into a paste with a little water, then add to a bowl filled with hot water. Soak your feet for 15 minutes. Ginger used in a similar way also promotes circulation and is warming in winter.

Salt water was Nanna's restorative for overworked feet. Take 2 basins, one containing very hot water and the other cold. Dissolve a handful of salt in each and give your feet alternate 10-second dips, as long as the water stays hot.

*See also Nervousness*

## FOXGLOVES

As well as providing a valuable stimulant for humans (the drug, *digitalis*), foxgloves seem to benefit other plants nearby. Adding foxglove leaves, or a tea made from the leaves, to a vase of cut flowers will help prolong their lives. No foxgloves handy? Wrap the entire vase and its contents loosely in moistened paper towelling or a dampened newspaper if you are worried about your arrangement drooping before a party. This trick also works well with sickly houseplants. Mignonette, on the other hand, is not a good companion for other cut flowers. If mignonette is placed in a vase, it will cause the other cut flowers present to wither and wilt very rapidly.

*See also Witches*

## FRAGRANCE

Smell is probably the most obvious way in which plants affect their vicinity. Most fragrances attract beneficial insects, such as bees, which pollinate flowers. Dandelions, on the other hand, exude a pungent and quite lethal ethylene gas, which inhibits the growth of nearby plants, causing them to mature and die over-early, thus giving the dandelion plenty of room to grow!

Similarly, as flower arrangers know, the ethylene gas emitted from bowls of picked fruit on a dining-room table will destroy any cut flowers in a vase in the same room. This is also why old wives would never store apples, pears or carrots together. Rather, they would occupy wooden baskets or barrels at opposite ends of the vast attics and cellars in old homes. Never mix apples with potatoes, either. The apples give the potatoes a bitter flavour and neither will keep well.

*See also Bee-youtiful Plants; Body Oil; Freshening The House; Jasmine; Potpourri*

## FRESHENING THE HOUSE

The simplest way to perfume the home is with pots or vases of sweet-scented flowers. Gather a few delicate roses, lavender and some crinkly green mint for a tiny cut-glass vase on the dressing table. Hang bunches of aromatic herbs, such as rosemary and woodruff, in the kitchen to keep the air cool and to deter flies. Twist fresh herbs and daisies into plaited rings and use them as serviette holders. Drop miniature bouquets of lemon verbena and geranium leaves into finger bowls for the dinner table.

*See also Potpourri*

## FROGS

Attract cheeping frogs to your garden with a small pond. As a bonus, they will eat lots of the pests that persecute your plants.

# FRUIT GROWING

In the home orchard, apricot trees should be underplanted with basil or southernwood, and peaches will thrive best if their neighbours include tansy and garlic. Grapes respond enthusiastically when hyssop is set about them.

*See also Citrus Trees; Fragrance; Garlic; Horseradish*

## GARLIC

Garlic planted amongst rose bushes helps keep aphids at bay. It is also a happy companion for most fruit trees. Set around the trunk, garlic deters borers and protects against various scab or scale infestations. Make a potent mosquito spray by infusing 4 crushed cloves of garlic in 1 litre (32 fl oz) of water. Spray the infusion around the garden. However, don't put garlic anywhere near strawberries, peas or beans, as it will inhibit their growth.

*See also Ants; Caterpillars; Cuts And Grazes; Fruit Growing; Romantic Roses*

## GERANIUMS

Brightly-coloured geraniums should be set amongst roses and grapevines to repel Japanese beetles, which can be a nuisance. They will also deter cabbage worms, if planted in the vegetable patch. Be sure to add a few geranium leaves to any potpourri mixture and to home-made jellies or jams, to add a pretty, spicy scent and flavour.

*See also Fertilisers; Freshening The House; Red Flowers; Scented Geraniums; Window Boxes*

## GHOST BUSTERS

Ghosts hate the golden flowers of St John's Wort, as do witches. A clump of any of the following herbs will repel both ghosts and witches, according to this old rhyme:

*Trefoile, vervain, herbe, jon, dylle,*
*Hinder wytches of theyre wylle.*

They would, however, be delighted to see hemlock in your garden, for they need to harvest the leaves to make their favourite flying ointment and noxious potions.

## GIFTS FROM YOUR GARDEN

When you harvest your herb garden, remember to pot up some cuttings as gifts. Be as generous as you can, for you will be delighted at the pleasure they will bring. House plants make cherished prizes and very personal gifts at any time of the year. A friend in hospital will enjoy a plant that is not only lovely to look at but also fragrant to smell and even delicious to nibble. Potted herbs are among the all-time best sellers at church fêtes, school fund-raising benefits, street markets or fairs. Get small terracotta pots and use some of the smaller plants for this purpose. (Never throw out those egg-cartons, either. They make admirable punnets for seedlings.) As the giver, you, too, will gain from this project, for you will enjoy the herbs lined up on the windowsill as they await gift days.

*See also Surprise Packets; Tussie-Mussies*

# HANDS

Your hands, like your lips, contain only a few sebaceous glands. This means the skin does not provide any lubrication and is therefore very prone to dryness. If they are very neglected, particularly in cold weather and after rough gardening work, your hands may actually crack and open the way for germs and inflammation. The first step in treating hands in this disastrous condition is to gently cleanse them of ingrained dirt. Here are several methods:

- A very simple and economical method is to massage your hands thoroughly with a gentle scrub made from raw sugar, sesame oil and lemon juice.
- Don't throw away squeezed-out lemon halves. Turned inside out and dipped in sugar, you can use them, mitt-style, on roughened ankles or elbows before applying a moisturising cream.
- The insides of avocado skins or a paste made with olive oil and rough salt are both very good for cleaning rough and grimy hands, as are ground almonds mixed with softened soap.

Follow your cleansing treatment with a good rub with more lemon juice, to remove stains (or freckles, if this is your problem). Wash your hands well in lukewarm water. Dry and massage them lavishly with cream or apply aloe vera gel, before pulling on cotton gloves and going to bed. Aloe vera, incidentally, is easy to grow as a houseplant. Try putting one in the kitchen. The marvellous healing gel is then close by, to quickly treat any burn or cut.

*See also Chapped Hands; Fingernails*

# HANGING BASKETS

The Elizabethans fastened earthenware pots of rosemary, which grows well indoors, to the outside of the chimney breast during summer, to keep the room cool and smelling sweet. Similarly, a basket of herbs, suspended over the kitchen sink, is an attractive and practical touch.

To prepare one, take a ready-made wire basket, about 45 cm (18 in) in diameter, and line it with sphagnum moss to absorb moisture. Then fill it with a mixture of soil, well blended with compost, and add a few pieces of charcoal, to prevent the basket smelling sour. Set the basket on top of another pot to work on. Plant with lemon balm, thyme and sweet basil as these all grow reasonably well indoors. For an elegant finish, plant a tiny-leafed ivy around the sides to trail gracefully. The grey-green leaves of these tiny ivies make a pretty addition to potpourri, too.

## HEADACHE

A handful of sweet marjoram, taken as an infusion in boiling water, is a good cure for a headache.

*See also Insect Repellents*

## HOLY PLANTS

The Madonna lily, with its holy aura, will keep ghosts from a garden and protect the virtue of the daughters of the house. Mimosa is a lucky flower and a charm against evil. Violets, spilling over a stone step, denote charity. Lavender is said to owe its pretty scent to the gentle ministrations of the Virgin Mary. Christian folk say she spread the infant Jesus' clothes on a lavender bush to dry and, in gratitude, she bestowed the shrub's sweet perfume. Christmas roses are another holy flower and, according to tradition, must always be planted near the front door, for this signifies that Christ is welcome within.

*See also Marigold; Oaks; Prayerful Plants; Spiritual Gardening; Witches*

## HONEYSUCKLE

Every garden should have at least one of the honeysuckles. Due to its habit of tightly embracing a support while pulling itself up towards sunlight, country folk have long called honeysuckle (or woodbine), 'love-bind' or 'hold-me-tight'. In Shakespeare's comedy, *A Midsummer Night's Dream*, the bewitched Titania takes Bottom in her arms and says, 'Sleep and I will wind thee in my arms ... so doth the sweet honeysuckle gently entwist ...' Elsewhere in the play, the spot where the Fairy Queen sits is described as:

*'... quite o'er canopied with luscious woodbine*
*With sweet musk roses and with eglantine ...'*

Perhaps Shakespeare was referring to his own sweetheart's garden, for those who have visited Anne Hathaway's cottage at Stratford-on-Avon know there is a small bower there, covered with twining honeysuckle stems.

Honeysuckles like a rich soil containing plenty of leaf mould, peat or bark fibre. Plant one on each

side of an archway, trellis or over the front door. They will climb together to the top and fill the air with their delicious perfume.

*See also Body Oil; Child's Play; Fairy Flora; Flowers As Food; Potpourri*

## HOPS

Golden hops will climb at least 2–3 metres (6½–10 ft) in just a single summer. Hops take their name from the Old English *hoppan*, meaning 'to climb', and their bright gold leaves look wonderful twisted around a trellis or post. To some, the scent of ripe hops acts as a relaxant and will induce deep sleep. (It is, after all, used in brewing alcoholic beverages, notably beer.) Pillows stuffed with newly-dried hops, lavender and rosemary are conducive to sound sleep. Hop tea, made by pouring boiling water on the flowers and allowing it to cool, will calm the nerves and tone the system if taken twice daily, between meals.

## HORSERADISH

Horseradish is one of the five 'bitter herbs' said to have been eaten by the Hebrews during Passover. It belongs to the same family as mustard and cress, meaning it is rich in sulphur and valuable as both a stimulant and a digestive. As a food, the grated, fresh root of horseradish is traditionally used as an accompaniment to roasted meat, grilled or baked fish and smoked foods. Freshly-grated horseradish perks up many vegetables and fruit dishes, from sauerkraut to apple sauce. Try it, if you don't believe it! Grated horseradish also releases a volatile oil, which is very useful for clearing head colds and sinus complaints. A poultice of grated horseradish may be applied externally to aching joints, for a similarly warming effect.

You can keep surplus horseradish roots fresh for months, either in the refrigerator or packed in damp sand. When you're ready to use them, try the following recipe.

## Horseradish Cream

Combine 1 cup (250 ml/8 fl oz) double cream, a squeeze of lemon juice and a touch of Dijon mustard. Grate 2.5 cm (1 in) fresh horseradish root, and add as much of it as is to your taste. Pour it into ice cube trays and freeze. The cubes will return to sauce state if you reheat them gently. Try as a dressing for pork satays or other grilled or roasted meats.

Peppery horseradish has long been used in folk medicine to treat throat infections and chronic catarrh. Similarly, planted next to potatoes or fruit trees, it will help cure any fungus. A tea made from horseradish leaves is effective against monilial infections in apple trees.

*See also Potatoes*

# HYSSOP

A blue-flowered hyssop hedge is a charming addition to a cottage-style garden and bees love its mint-flavoured leaves. Planted near grape vines, hyssop will increase their yield, but if it is near radishes, it will curl their toes.

*See also Bee-youtiful Plants; Fruit Growing; Window Boxes*

# INSECT REPELLENTS

There are several ornamental herbs with attractive flowers which act as natural insect repellents, including asters, cosmos, autumn chrysanthemums, pyrethrum and coreopsis. The dainty old-fashioned feverfew flower— much used by herbalists for treating migraines and headaches—is effective in deterring flies, gnats and other winged pests, as are yarrow, lavender, artemisia and lavender cotton (*santolina*).

See also *Ants; Basil; Bay Leaves; Caterpillars; Marigold; Mosquitoes; Moth Deterrents; Nasturtiums; Strawberries; Tansy*

# INSOMNIA

Lettuce is an old gypsy remedy against sleeplessness, being soothing and mildly laxative. Lettuce tea, drunk at bedtime, is an excellent cure for constipation. Valerian (from the Latin *valere*, to be healthy) is another strong herb which the gypsies used to induce sleep, along with southernwood, which was claimed to cure hysteria. Girls would once use southernwood and lovage as love charms, to win the attention of young men.

Old country folk also knew that an infusion of elder flowers, taken last thing at night, would soothe the spirit of a nervous patient who was unable to sleep. Similarly, warmed elderberry wine, served with a little ginger, is a recipe for sound sleep on a winter's night.

# IVY

It is lucky to plant green or variegated ivy around the front door, as it protects those within from misfortune. (Ugly, brown, wrinkled dwarves and goblins are said to especially dislike ivy.) If the ivy dies, however, the Welsh say this means the house will soon be sold.

Ivy has always been a popular choice for decorating walls, fences and rockeries. Its firmly clasping habit was once considered a lucky love charm. A girl would place three ivy leaves in her pocket when out, in the certain belief that the first fellow who spoke to her would become her husband.

Quick-growing and bright, its young leaves tipped with gold flecks, one of the prettiest ivies is *Hedera angularis* 'Aurea'. Also very attractive is the more common *Hedera canariensis* 'Variegata', which has large, pointed leaves, splashed with silver and gold.

*See also Hanging Baskets*

# JASMINE

In his *Records of the Plants of Southern China*, Chi Han, writing in the 3rd century AD, described the city of Canton at the height of the jasmine season as being '... like snow at night, fragrant everywhere. The flowers were used in making perfumes and scented oils to rub on the body. Indeed, everyone had the delicious scent about them.'

As befits a plant with such exotic oriental origins, the dainty flowers of the white jasmine, *Jasminum officinale*, have a luscious perfume which stirs the senses. Elizabethan poets mention it as being in common use on arbours even then, for it was introduced from the East during Tudor times.

White jasmine is best planted from pots in spring. It will grow 3–4 m (10–13 ft) within 2 years. If jasmine plants are set at both sides of a bower, they will soon meet overhead, where the sprays of white flowers are so attractive against the masses of small, dark-green leaves. Jasmine normally makes plenty of twiggy growth. The stems should be interlaced with the trellis or other support. Tie it, as necessary, while it grows. It should be planted in a sheltered, warm position, because the leaves can be damaged by excessive cold.

Ordinary soil suits jasmine quite well and, for added protection, plant rosemary or lavender around its base. To increase jasmine's heady fragrance, in early summer set one of the night-scented tobacco plants, *Nicotiana affinis* or *Verbena teucriodes* nearby. Brazilian girls claim the pinky-white flowers of the latter are a potent aphrodisiac, and thread them through their hair in the evenings.

*See also Body Oil; Body Powders*

> THE KISS OF THE SUN FOR PARDON
> THE SONGS OF THE BIRDS FOR MIRTH;
> YOU ARE NEARER GOD'S HEART IN A GARDEN
> THAN ANYWHERE ELSE ON THIS EARTH.
>
> TRADITIONAL

## KIDNEY PROBLEMS

Herbalists claim that Librans are especially prone to kidney and skin disorders. Gypsy lore endorses this and herbs ruled by Venus and Libra are usually diuretic. For instance, yarrow flowers and pennyroyal, which may be used in salads, are both warming, tonic herbs with a pronounced diuretic effect. An infusion of sweet violets is a gypsy remedy for kidney and bladder pain. It has strong antiseptic and purgative qualities, so should only be taken in moderation.

## KNEES

A kneeling pad is a must-have for any gardener, to reduce stiffness and prevent contact with any rash-causing weeds. An old hot-water bottle may be loosely filled with sand, then popped in an old pillowslip to make a marvellous kneeling pad.

HE THAT HATH A GOOD HARVEST MUST BE CONTENT
TO HAVE SOME THISTLES, TOO.

## LADYBIRD

Don't shoo any ladybird in your garden to 'fly away home'. They eat an incredible number of aphids and mealybugs and, being able to penetrate areas often inaccessible to sprays, are a gardener's best friend.

*See also Aphids; Parsley*

## LAVENDER

Ensure a healthy, well-shaped lavender bush with regular hard pruning in autumn. This process will produce flowers over a much longer period. Always be sure to leave green wood below the trim line and don't clip the old wood. Don't waste the prunings, either. The leaves should be stripped and put into a large earthenware jar, in preparation for making potpourri. Otherwise, you could throw them on the barbecue to add a new flavour dimension to food. Rather than just include lavender as part of the muddle in a mixed flower bed, try one of these more imaginative ideas:

- Build a specially-raised bed of brick or stone and set a seat in the side where the lavender is planted. The aroma will then be closer to nose level.
- Fill the paths with mauve-coloured pebbles, as was the fashion in Tudor times, or plant your lavender with low-growing chamomile. Place a favourite stone birdbath or sundial nearby, to attract feathered friends.
- Plant lavender, chamomile and peppermint in a hanging basket. Place it by the barbecue area or in that special spot where you might like to sit on a warm night. The aroma helps to repel insects.

For centuries, gardeners have regarded lavender as a 'good' companion, repelling all fly pests, millipedes and some slugs. Plant it by tomatoes, cabbages and carrots, to encourage good crops. An old wives' tale has it that primulas and crocus—elsewhere usually ruined by birds and bugs—are left untouched growing beside a

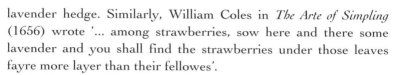

lavender hedge. Similarly, William Coles in *The Arte of Simpling* (1656) wrote '... among strawberries, sow here and there some lavender and you shall find the strawberries under those leaves fayre more layer than their fellowes'.

The lavender bush, with its grey-green foliage and fragrant flowers, is a favourite in older-style cottage gardens. A bonus is that lavender in bloom attracts bees and other nectar-seeking insects, which will pollinate all the other flowers nearby. The Roman poet, Virgil, said beehives should be ' ... in beds of fresh lavender and stores of wild thyme, with strong savory to flower'. Honey from hives located amidst flowers has a sublime taste. No one who has tasted it could ask for sweeter. Lavender's warm, evocative fragrance made it a favourite culinary herb in older times. It was crystallised as a sweetmeat and used to mask the gamey taste of ill-preserved meat, while Elizabeth I delighted in a certain 'lavender conserve' and used it liberally as a relish. Lavender may be used to make a variety of cosmetic aids, such as mouthwash, skin tonics and eye lotions. Rinsing the complexion with sweet lavender water, especially that made with rain or spring water, has long been believed to beautify the skin.

## Lavender and Rosemary Toner

*20 lavender flowers*
*2 tablespoons rosemary leaves*
*125 ml (4 fl oz) witch hazel*
*125 ml (4 fl oz) distilled or spring water*
*few drops of peppermint oil (optional)*


Infuse the herbs in water and witch hazel in a covered, non-aluminium saucepan, over low heat, for 5 minutes. Remove from the heat and leave to cool. Strain, pressing down well on the flowers, and add peppermint oil if desired. Decant into an atomiser or glass-stoppered bottle.

*See also Astral Daze; Bee-youtiful Plants; Bruises; Fever; Freshening The House; Holy Plants; Insect Repellents; Mosquitoes; Nervousness; Potpourri; Strawberries; Vinegars; Violets; Window Boxes*

THUNDER IN SPRING, THE COLD IT WILL BRING.

## LEATHER

Never throw out any old leather boots or shoes. Bury them instead. They will rot surprisingly quickly, releasing valuable nutrients into the soil.

## LEEK-Y ROOF?

The Welsh love the tiny house-leek and say that if it is found growing on a roof, it will protect that house from lightning and storms. A 16th century writer said, '... houseleke growth in muntaynes and hylly places and some use it set upon theyr houses ...' No doubt any roof damp enough to support plants would not readily go up in flames as a result of a lightning strike anyway.

*See also Carrots*

## LEMON BALM

Also known as 'bee balm' because of its sweet scent which is beloved by bees, lemon balm leaves may be added to chilled summer drinks or used to make a pleasantly soothing tea. Any savoury dish which could normally be flavoured with lemon juice can also be enhanced with lemon balm. Try adding a few leaves to fish sauces or veal stuffing. It is also superb with fruity desserts.

*See also Bee-youtiful Plants; Hanging Baskets; Nervousness*

# LEMONY LOVELINESS

The tangy lemon is one of the world's oldest and most useful fruits and the trees feature in many suburban gardens. There are many different varieties, the main ones being Eureka, Villa Franca and Meyer. There are also some rather eccentric types, such as the American Wonder Lemon, with fruit weighing up to 1 kg (2 lb) each (!) and the Turk's Head, said to bear fruit the size of a man's head.

The lemon makes a most attractive bush or small tree. The small, white flowers are tinged with pinky-red when they are just new and they are extremely fragrant, their soft, rich, heavy scent acting as a magnet for birds and bees. Lemons do not require a very deep or rich soil in order to flourish. Nor do they enjoy over-watering and they loathe having boggy feet. Never puddle the soil around a new arrival. This will cause the soil to cake and pack too densely and thus prevent the roots being able to spread. One of the most common causes of failure when growing lemon trees is 'collar rot', when close, moist conditions cause the bark to lift from the base of the trunk. Similarly, lemon trees should be fed with great care. Many are killed or damaged by an enthusiastic gardener, who is concerned about lack of fruit. Like many citrus trees, lemons are usually unproductive until the main branches have matured.

The lemon has a long tradition of use as a home medicine. The Romans dosed pregnant women with lemon cordials, according to Pliny, '... to stay flux and vomit'. The juice makes an excellent gargle for a sore throat and, being a rich source of vitamins C and P, it will help maintain the health of the skin, strengthening the

tiny capillaries seen near the surface. Lemon juice has a wonderful toning effect and mild deodorant properties.

With all the following recipes, strain the lemon juice before using it. Try to buy or use organically grown lemons, rather than those which have been treated with pesticides, for your skin or hair. Better still, grow your own. Even the busiest city-dweller can look after a potted lemon tree on a sunny balcony.

### Tingling Toner
A simple astringent may be made by mixing together 2 tablespoons of witch hazel, 6 tablespoons of rosewater and 1 teaspoon of lemon juice.

### Lemon Mask for Sallow Skin
Add the juice of 3 lemons to a strong brew of chamomile tea. Stir in powdered skim milk until you have a thick, gritty texture. Apply to clean, damp skin, avoiding the delicate eye area, and lie down for 15 minutes as the mask dries. Rinse off with lukewarm water.

### Hair Lightening Paste
To an infusion of chamomile tea, add the juice of a lemon and enough kaolin powder to form a paste. Work through your hair and leave for 1 hour before rinsing out. The process can be speeded up if you dry the paste with a hair dryer or sit out in the sunshine while it's on.

*See also Citrus Trees; Hands; Preserving Flowers And Plants*

## LETTUCE
Practically every gardener has tried to grow lettuce, thinking it should be easy. It's not. Lettuce needs plenty of water and nearly all garden pests just love it. Wood ash sprinkled over surrounding soil will help to keep insects away, as will interplanting with marigolds.

Lettuce grows particularly well with strawberries, cucumbers and carrots, and radishes grown with lettuce always seem to be juicier than usual.

*See also Chamomile; Insomnia; Radishes; Romantic Roses; Strawberries*

## LIFE INDICES

The emperors of the Manchu dynasty of China took the air in a tiny private garden, in the Forbidden City of Peking, where all the trees were clipped into formal shapes except for one — the *Life Tree* of the dynasty. This was allowed to sprawl, unchecked, for the wellbeing and continuance of the royal house was thought to depend upon its abundant growth.

In 19th century Switzerland, an apple tree was planted for the birth of a boy, a pear for a girl, and the child was thought to languish or flourish according to the tree's progress. Thus, planting a tree is almost like life insurance. The owner can expect to absorb the tree's vitality and longevity into his or her own life pattern.

Many trees seem prophetically attuned to coming events. One of the best-authenticated life-index stories attaches to the Kemperfelt family. Admiral Richard Kemperfelt and his brother, Gustavus, both planted commemorative thorn trees at their home in England. Later, when the admiral was away with the fleet, Gustavus noticed that Richard's thorn had withered suddenly and died. He expressed fears for his brother's safety, and that evening (August 29, 1782) came the news of the disastrous sinking of the admiral's ship, with the loss of 'twice four hundred men'.

Another practice, akin to life indices, holds that as soon as a young child can walk, it should be carried into the garden and set down. The first plant it touches will reveal the character of its future life. If, for example, the plant touched is rosemary, the child may look forward to a life of happiness; if a lily of the valley, of humility and purity; thyme, a single life; and sage, a life of wisdom. All these predictions are based on the ancient reputations and infective magic of garden plants.

TREFOIL AND CLOVER WILL CONTRACT THEIR PETALS AT THE APPROACH OF A HEAVY STORM. MARIGOLDS BEHAVE IN A SIMILAR MANNER.

## LILAC LUCK

White lilac and May blossom are unlucky when brought into a house, but quite safe (and very pretty) when planted in a garden. In fact, purple lilacs, planted in rows at the corners of a house, will protect against evil spirits. If planted in pairs, make sure you favour each lilac bush equally, for they are very jealous. Also, avoid cutting just one, for the other will pine and remain flowerless for an entire season, in sympathy.

## LIME BLOSSOM

Lime blossom is lucky for a new, young wife with a meddling mother-in-law. She could be assured that a brew of valerian, skullcap and lime blossom, freshly gathered from the garden, would turn the in-law's criticism to kindness.

## LUNGWORT

Lungwort is a dear little herb. As its name indicates, country folk held it in great esteem for treating 'chestiness', coughs and sneezes. Another old remedy for chest conditions and rheumatism linked with cold and damp, was a syrup made from lungwort and rosehips. Gypsies would regularly harvest bright red rose hips, come winter, and prepare them with dried lungwort leaves, to make a potent syrup. Rich in vitamins A and C, this would help to ward off winter ills and colds.

## MARIGOLD

Pretty marigolds, which are variously known as 'marybuds', 'marygolds', 'gold ruddes' or, more simply, 'golds', owe their many names to their association with the Virgin Mary—hence the introduction of 'marigold petal' windows in ladies' chapels in medieval England.

At one time, the flowers were called 'pot marigolds', due to their culinary properties. The petals were often served as a cheap substitute for saffron and were used to impart a savoury tang to stews, broths and cheeses. The fresh petals are delicious in salads or you can try your hand at a marigold pudding, made by combining chopped petals, lemon juice and grated lemon zest with soft white breadcrumbs. Marigold flowers add flavour and interest to sweet dishes, too. Try including them with stewed fruits, such as plums and rhubarb, in winter time. Whip crushed marigold petals through natural yoghurt or soft, white cheese and top with chopped chives, for a more savoury treat.

Dried and finely crumbled, marigold petals will add colour and flavour to noodles, rice and soups. To dry, place the petals on a sheet of foil and bake them in a slow oven until crisp. You might like to try the following recipe for marigold mayonnaise. This makes a very decorative talking point with sliced tomatoes and cucumbers or with avocados stuffed with seafood.

## Marigold Mayonnaise

*24 fresh marigold blooms*
*250 g (8 oz) natural, thick mayonnaise*
*juice ½ lemon*
*6 teaspoons cream*
*salt and freshly ground pepper*
*dash of paprika*

Place all ingredients in a blender and whirl at high speed for 1 minute. Garnish with 1 or 2 whole marigold flowers.

By the way, both the colour and scent of marigolds are believed to repel harmful insects or other pests. My mother claims they discourage nematodes in the soil. Similarly, marigolds are an excellent companion to tomatoes in the home garden, as they deter asparagus beetle and tomato worm.

*See also Bee Stings; Dyepot From Nature; Nematodes; Potpourri; Red Flowers; Spells*

## MARROWS

Plant a single pumpkin amongst your marrows and, it is said, your marrow crop will treble.

## MATCHES

Potted plants, such as orchids, often fail to flower despite constant care and attention. Scanning an old gardening book, I came across a tip from a nurseryman who specialised in growing ornamental flowering plants in pots, especially bulbs and tubers. His theory went something like this: these plants are greedy mineral feeders and can rapidly deplete their potting mix of sulphates, so put a boxful of match heads into the soil, rake them in with your fingers and water in the usual way. He claimed great success with this method, maintaining that the plants would not stop flowering as a result.

## MEDIEVAL METHODS

Henry VIII's gardener customarily left a branch of each fruit tree uncut at pruning time, to 'cherish the sap'. This was possibly derived from a folk memory of appeasing the tree's spirit for such disrespectful interference.

His daughter, Elizabeth I, was especially fond of scented carnation pinks ('gillyflowers' as they were then known). Her gardeners were wont to steep the seeds in sweetened milk before sowing them, in the hope of growing an even more fragrant variety, to please their fastidious mistress.

## MILK

When rinsing out milk bottles, always shake up the residue with a little warm water and pour this over the garden. It is an excellent mild fertiliser.

## MINT SOURCE

In addition to its culinary merits, mint was strewn on kitchen floors to repel vermin and it figured as a tithing herb in the Bible. It should never be cut with an iron instrument or misfortune will result. Nor should the seeds or cuttings be bought or sold. The best results are said to ensue when the plants are given from one gardener to another, preferably with a gracious little speech.

Within this group of refreshing, cooling herbs, many different varieties have been cultivated since very ancient times. The Greeks and Romans crowned themselves with peppermint at banquets and placed bunches on tables. Mints were a popular strewing herb in medieval England, where they were used in dark, fusty church pews and great halls. Long ago, it was known that mice and rats hate the smell of mint, so it was often grown near food crops to deter vermin. Bees, on the other hand, love mint and apiarists would rub it inside hives. In fact, old-time *herbwyfes* recommended rubbing bee and wasp stings with cooling mint leaves.

Pennyroyal, *Mentha pulegium*, is one of the prettiest ground covers in the garden. It is dense and extremely sturdy and bears

dainty little mauve flower spikes
in summer. (If it has a fault, it is in
being so vigorous as to be intrusive.
Unchecked, it will spread right
through a garden, popping up
in flower beds or cracks in the
driveway.) Pennyroyal can be used
to great effect as a lawn, either by
itself, or mixed with sweeps of other
mints, like peppermint (*Mentha
piperita*), spearmint (*Mentha spicata*)
and apple mint (*Mentha sauveolens*).
Another idea is to mould a 'couch' from
earth, in a shady nook in the garden,
and plant it all over with clumps of
pennyroyal. Not only will such a pretty
spot refresh the senses, it will also repel
flies. If you do not want mint to spread
all over your garden, confine the roots
beneath the ground. Either sink an old
bath or deep trough into the ground and
grow the mint in that, or sink a fence of
upended bricks or old-fashioned terracotta
edging tiles around the mint patch.

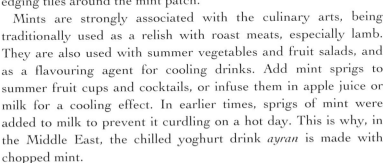

Mints are strongly associated with the culinary arts, being
traditionally used as a relish with roast meats, especially lamb.
They are also used with summer vegetables and fruit salads, and
as a flavouring agent for cooling drinks. Add mint sprigs to
summer fruit cups and cocktails, or infuse them in apple juice or
milk for a cooling effect. In earlier times, sprigs of mint were
added to milk to prevent it curdling on a hot day. This is why, in
the Middle East, the chilled yoghurt drink *ayran* is made with
chopped mint.

All the mints are highly digestive, especially peppermint, so they
will ease troubled tummies, hiccups and nausea. Mints were an
important ingredient in many early dentifrices, while peppermint
tea was used to prevent giddiness, as were lavender smelling salts.

## Peppermint Tea

Peppermint tea is equally refreshing served hot or icy cold, garnished with lemon twists and lots of extra mint sprigs. Use 1 teaspoon of dried peppermint leaves per cup and 1 for the pot.

Put the peppermint in a china or glass teapot, pour boiling water over and allow it to infuse for about 2–3 minutes, to taste. Strain and add a little honey or a squeeze of lemon juice, if desired.

## Mint Jelly

To make mint jelly, wash and quarter 6–8 of the earliest unripe apples (these contain more pectin). Put them, seeds and all, into a non-aluminium saucepan, just cover them with water and boil until they are reduced to a pulp. Strain

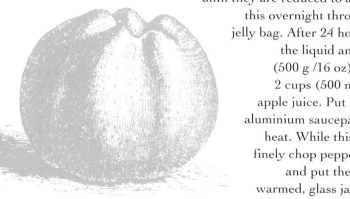

this overnight through a muslin jelly bag. After 24 hours, measure the liquid and add 2 cups (500 g /16 oz) of sugar per 2 cups (500 ml/16 fl oz) of apple juice. Put this in a non-aluminium saucepan over a low heat. While this is warming, finely chop peppermint leaves and put them into clean, warmed, glass jars. When the apple jelly is just at setting point, carefully fill each jar. Stir the mint through the jelly severaltimes while it is setting, so it is evenly distributed. When the jelly has cooled slightly, seal and label the jars.

## Mint Butter

A delicious mint butter may be used as a garnish for grilled steak or lamb chops. For 250 g (8 oz) of butter, prepare 4 tablespoons of chopped mint. Soften the butter and gradually mash through the mint and 1 teaspoon of lemon juice. Put the butter on

greaseproof paper and shape it into a roll or press it into a decorative mould. Place it in the refrigerator to harden.

See also Ants; Bee Stings; Chamomile; Freshening The House; Lavender; Moth Deterrents; Muscle Soreness; Paths; Pennyroyal; Strawberries; Vinegars

## MISTLETOE

Long associated with love and romance, many ancient tales attend the parasitic mistletoe. It was highly revered—even feared—by the mystic Druids of old, who believed the white berries contained the host tree's seminal fluid and, therefore, used them as a symbol of fertility and rebirth in their magic rituals. This is one explanation for mistletoe's traditional use to 'deck the halls' at Christmas time. Another legend has it that when the Norse god, Balder, was slain, the goddess Freya wept over his body and her tears brought him back to life. The droplets crystallised into mistletoe berries which, henceforth, became emblematic of love and compassion.

IN SCOTLAND, AT THE FULL MOON, PEOPLE CUT BRANCHES OF MISTLETOE AND WEAVE THEM INTO CIRCULAR WREATHS, WHICH THEY KEEP ALL YEAR ROUND AS A CHARM AGAINST ILLNESS.

## MOODS

'Green thumb' folklore continually emphasises the fact that plants respond to human personality. Bad temper is as injurious to them as happiness is elating. A gardener's black moods may come again, to plague those who eat vegetables he or she planted on a bad day. Positive gardeners must contribute love, happiness and strength to their gardens. These qualities, in partnership with both practical attention to the requirements of compost and water and emanations from soil and cosmos, ensure success.

See also Music; Talking to Plants

# MOONSTRUCK

For best results, mystically-oriented botanists will tell you that plants should only be pruned when the moon is waxing, for if pruned when it is waning, they will wither completely. Scientists have now caught up with this, discovering that the effects of lunar rhythms on the earth's magnetic field do, in fact, affect growth. They have established that water everywhere—including that inside the tiniest leaf—moves in tides, like the sea. The moon also affects the earth's atmosphere so that, statistically, it is more likely to rain heavily (just as you would like it to) immediately after planting during a full or new moon. They also say that a potato grown under constant heat and light in laboratory conditions will still manage to show a growth rhythm that reflects the lunar pattern.

SHE CERTAINLY CHOPPED OFF THE DANDELION'S HEAD, BUT THERE WAS MORE TO FOLLOW. TAKING A SMALL, SHARP, STEEL INSTRUMENT, SHE BORED A HOLE IN ITS BLEEDING TRUNK AND INJECTED A DROP OF STRONG POISON, SAYING IN A QUIET, ICY-COLD VOICE, 'THERE YOU ARE MY DEAR; HOW DO YOU LIKE THAT? DO COME AGAIN AND HAVE SOME MORE.'
THIS WAS THE WOMAN'S WAY, DONE WITH SO MUCH PATIENCE AND CARE.
BEING A MAN, I JUST CHOP THE HEAD OFF SAVAGELY, WITH A CRY OF, 'TAKE THAT, YOU SWINE!'

QUOTED IN **W. H. DAVIES**, MY GARDEN (1933)

## MOSQUITOES

Oddly enough, male gardeners are more likely to be attacked by mosquitoes. Older men generally suffer three times as many bites as younger men, four times as many as women and about ten times as many as young children. Wear white or pale shades of pink or green to reduce your mosquito-attraction potential. They seem to be most attracted to black, red, bright blue and dark floral prints.

Give mozzies a scented send-off. Dabbing lavender oil on with a cotton ball works like a charm. So does crushing a handful of pennyroyal leaves and rubbing them onto your skin. Or, try sweet aniseed oil (what you don't use, you can pop in with your next batch of biscuits!). If you don't mind smelling like 'Eau de Shallot', dab straight onion juice onto your skin. It's a very effective personal insect repellent. You might also like to try using a tea made out of one of the bug-beating repellent herbs, such as southernwood, rue, lemongrass or wormwood. Sprinkle the liquid on your hat or clothing or tie a handkerchief, moistened in the liquid, loosely around your neck. Here's a very old country trick. Wrap old-fashioned fly-paper around the rim of your hat! No doubt you won't win the local fashion stakes, but you'll be surprised at the number of 'occupants' the fly paper will have at the end of the day—and you will have avoided the use of any poisonous repellents.

If the mosquitoes do get to you before you get to the pennyroyal or lavender, reduce the sting with lecithin oil, available from most pharmacies. Simply pierce a capsule and rub the contents onto the mosquito bite to reduce redness and itching.

*See also Garlic*

## MOTH DETERRENTS

Placing scented sachets between piles of sheets and towels in the linen press will fill them with fragrance. The best moth deterrent of all is a combination of crushed bay leaves, camphor and lavender. Other old-fashioned moth preventives for you to harvest from your garden include peppermint, rosemary, spearmint, tansy and sweet woodruff. Either pack into sachets and fold amongst your linen, or scatter powdered mix directly onto shelves.

*See also Bay Leaves; Sage Advice*

## MULBERRIES

Birds love mulberries and there should always be enough fruit to spare for feathered friends. Once attracted to a garden, birds will eat troublesome garden pests. Mulberry trees are good companions for grape-vines. Tree-grown grapes may be a bit more difficult to pick but are always healthier and free from fungal diseases, presumably because of the better air circulation around them.

By the way, do you know the best way to remove telltale mulberry stains from children's clothes? Odd though it may sound, you should rub the stain with an *unripe* mulberry, which seems to neutralise it.

## MUSCLE SORENESS

Despite your warm-up exercises (see page 38) you may still have done yourself an injury in the garden. Many common and familiar herbs and plants form simple remedies to help relieve muscle soreness and other ailments. The leaves of any of these plants may be bruised and bound onto a sprain: agrimony, mallow, St John's Wort and vervain. A warm, soothing compress can be made by softening the leaves in a sieve held over boiling water, then pulping and applying them as a poultice.

Rosemary is also excellent for relieving stiff joints and relaxing aching muscles. It was used by Roman soldiers to relieve their tired feet after a long march. Other sweet-smelling herbs can be blended in any combination to your personal taste to provide a tonic effect in the bath, helping to ease aching muscles and joints. These include marjoram, basil, meadowsweet and pennyroyal. In particular, spearmint is a tonic for body and soul. Try a spearmint bath for a wonderfully invigorating start to a fine spring day's gardening!

## MMMM—MUSHROOMS

*When the moon is in the full*
*Mushrooms you may freely pull;*
*But when the moon is on the wane*
*Wait 'ere you think to pluck again.*

### Piquant Mushrooms

*350 g (12 oz) mushrooms*
*chicken or vegetable stock, to cover*
*1 cup (250 ml/8 fl oz) sour cream*
*2 tablespoons grated horseradish*
*2 tablespoons chopped parsley*
*1 tablespoon crushed garlic*
*1 teaspoon Dijon mustard*
*freshly ground black pepper and salt*

Preheat the oven to 180°C. Lightly butter a baking dish. Combine the mushrooms and stock in a large pot, bring it to the boil and cook for 8–10 minutes, or until tender. Make a sauce by blending together the sour cream, vinegar, horseradish, parsley, garlic and mustard. Add salt and pepper, to taste. Drain the mushrooms and arrange them in a baking dish, cover with sauce and bake for 10–15 minutes. Serve hot.

SOW DRY AND SET IN THE WET.

IF DRY BE THE BUCK'S HORN ON HOLYROOD MORN (SEPTEMBER 14)
IT'S WORTH A CHEST OF GOLD;
BUT IF WET BE SEEN ON HOLYROOD E'EN
BAD HARVEST IS FORESEEN.

TRADITIONAL YORKSHIRE SAYING

## MUSIC

Many people find their plants respond to music and song. The owner of a local nursery believes that plants appreciate classical and oriental music, particularly Wagner and the sitar.

A growing body of scientific data illumines such convictions. Experiments include those of Dr T. Singh, from Madras University. He asked a friend to play his stringed *veena* to a group of *Impatiens balsamina*. After the fifth week of music, the balsams which had listened to the *veena* had 72 per cent more leaves and were 20 per cent taller than the controls.

Other experiments show that raucous music is disliked by plants. After two weeks, one group of marigolds hearing rock music had died. An identical group, only 2 m (6½ ft) away but listening to classical music, was thriving. Rock-

stimulated plants demanded far greater quantities of water than the classical group and their roots were stunted by comparison.

## MYRTLE

Myrtle should be planted on either side of the front verandah, preferably by the woman of the house, to ensure that peace and love reign within.

IF YOU CAN CATCH A FALLING LEAF BEFORE IT REACHES THE GROUND, YOU WILL HAVE TWELVE MONTHS OF GOOD LUCK.

## NASTURTIUMS

Originally admired for its attractive flowers and easy growth, the nasturtium's culinary applications have also been explored. The flowers, leaves and seed pods are all edible and flavoursome, with a subtle peppery taste. Pick the flowers when they are fully open but still fresh. They make an attractive garnish for soups, puréed vegetables or smoked salmon. A particularly delightful idea is to fill the flowers with a cream cheese and pineapple mixture and serve them as hors d'oevres. I also like the idea of a nasturtium pâté, made by blending finely-chopped nasturtiums (flowers and leaves) with cream cheese and a dash of paprika. Serve with vegetables as a dip, or on hot toast as a spread.

The cress-like mild flavour of the leaves combines well with many foods. Try mixing chopped nasturtium leaves into a bean and green-onion salad or a plate of fresh cucumbers, seasoned with a pinch of snipped chives. Minced nasturtium leaves make a subtle garnish for chilled cream soups or you can combine them with chives to flavour a fresh omelette.

The seed pods should be picked when tiny and green, just after the flower has withered. When pickled in vinegar, they taste very much like capers. Add them to a sauce of butter, crumbled blue cheese and lemon juice and serve over steamed vegetables. Alternatively, chop them up finely and add to mayonnaise, to make a delicious sauce for fish.

### Pickled Nasturtium Seeds

*50 g (1½ oz) nasturtium seeds*
*50 g (1½ oz) horseradish, grated*
*4 or 5 shallots, finely minced*
*5 cloves*
*50 g (1½ oz) black peppercorns*
*1 mace blade*
*pinch grated nutmeg*
*1 tablespoon white mustard seeds*

75 g (2½ oz) sea salt or rock salt
water
300 ml (10 fl oz) white wine vinegar
75 ml (2½ fl oz) fresh lime or lemon juice

Place the seeds in a sterile glass jar, sprinkle them with salt and add enough cold water to cover them. Cap the jar securely and store it in a cool, dry place for 1 week, shaking it occasionally. Drain the seeds and combine them with the horseradish, shallots, cloves, peppercorns, mace, nutmeg and mustard seeds in a non-aluminium saucepan. Pour the vinegar and lime or lemon juice over them and simmer for 10–12 minutes. Do not boil. Pour the mixture into warmed, sterile jars, label and cap them securely.

Nasturtiums repel a wide range of harmful insects from fruit and vegetables, whether planted nearby or used in an organic spray. They secrete a mustardy oil which aphids, in particular, find unattractive, so it makes good sense to let them ramble amongst your crops of cabbage, kohlrabi or turnips. In fact, as the flowers, seeds and leaves of the nasturtium are all edible, it should take its place in the vegetable garden on its own merits, anyway. Nasturtiums also improve the growth and flavour of neighbouring crops, especially radishes, which tend to have a more peppery flavour as a result.
   *See also Aphids; Cabbages; Red Plants; Tomatoes; Zucchini*

PLANT CHILIES WHILE YOU ARE ANGRY. IT WILL
MAKE THEM COME UP QUICKER AND THEY WILL
BE HOTTER TO THE TASTE. IF YOU ARE PICKLING
YOUR CHILIES AND WISH THEM TO BE MILD,
HAVE THEM CLEANED AND SALTED BY A PERSON
WITH A MILD DISPOSITION.

## NATURE SPIRITS

Using organic methods on ground swept by gales and composed largely of dust and gravel, the Scottish Findhorn community grows well over 65 varieties of vegetables, 21 of fruits and 40 of herbs. Visitors have expressed astonishment at the crops. A cabbage, normally weighing about 1.8 kg (4 lb), reached *19 kg (42 lb)* in weight. A delphinium, growing in pure sand, reached a height of 2.5 m (8 ft) and roses customarily bloom amidst snow and ice.

After deep meditation, the community members received instructions to communicate with the *devas*, the higher architects of plant life who control nature spirits and with whom, it is said, gardeners with 'green thumbs' are unconsciously in communication. Mystical exchanges have had practical results. When neighbouring paths became overgrown with gorse, for example, it was explained to the *devas* that the community's walks were being spoiled. The following year, no gorse grew upon the paths.

## NEMATODES

The roots of certain herbs and plants can exude substances which assist (or hinder) the growth of others nearby, or which kill or repel pests that would otherwise attack these neighbours. For instance, the chemical secretions from the roots of marigolds, grown over a full season, will help kill ground elder and bindweed and also be effective in nematode control. These horrid little parasites destroy the roots of many vegetables, including

tomatoes, capsicums, chilies and eggplants. To clear nematode-infested soil before planting any of these crops, put in marigolds, then dig them back into the soil at the end of their flowering season. Other plants which exude a natural nematicide include dahlias, asparagus and some salvias.

*See also Cucumbers; Marigold*

## NERVOUSNESS
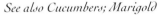

An old remedy for nervousness was to put a spot of lavender oil on a lump of sugar and suck it. Oil of lavender may also be used in a warm water foot bath to relieve aching feet or as an infusion for a facial steam. A syrup made from lemon balm can give comfort to a nervy stomach and agrimony has long been used to treat diarrhoea induced by nervousness. Fennel is a strong plant with a strong flavour, particularly indicated for the faint-hearted. Roman gardeners sprinkled it over their food to give them courage, so it is ideal for a nervous patient. Barley is also appropriate for those suffering nervous distress or fever. It is rich in magnesium, making it an excellent nerve tonic. Mashed barley, pounded together with figs, raisins and liquorice root, is a sure cure for constipation.

## NETTLES

Don't be too hasty in dismissing this weed. It may be unsightly and the stinging hairs are certainly unfriendly, but it is also a versatile medicinal herb and its uses as a food abound. Something like spinach, young nettle leaves are quite a delicacy in the spring. Nettles are rich in chlorophyll and protein, vitamins A and C and minerals such as iron and phosphorus.

Nettles have many uses in the garden and their presence actually indicates a good soil, rich in nitrogen. They make excellent companion plants, especially for herbs, by increasing the quantity of essential oils found in plants growing nearby. They may also help their neighbours resist disease. Although you may be tempted to pull them up, they do assist in the formation of humus. If, however, you simply can't bear to see them amongst your

carefully-tended plants, throw them onto the compost heap or use them for mulch once they have dried. Nettles are invaluable in the organic garden instead of artificial fertilisers, for their high nitrogen content is welcome by all plants. They definitely shouldn't be wasted.

Nettles secrete silica, iron and protein into the soil, thus strengthening nearby crops. Tomatoes, in particular, would be sorry to see any neighbouring nettles go. Nettles should be placed in layers in compost. The carbonic acid and ammonia in the leaves will hasten the fermentation of the rest of the plant material. Ground-up nettle leaves in their mash will cause hens to lay more, and bigger, eggs. Nettles also keep snails and slugs away, especially during wet weather.

Nettles are much used by herbalists in the treatment of blood, lung and circulatory disorders. In fact, nettles have more iron than any other land plant. This makes them a wonderful blood tonic and cleanser. Nettles can be taken internally as a tea or used as a spring vegetable in a variety of ways. A course of nettle tea in the early days of spring will help shake off winter sluggishness, by invigorating and strengthening the system. (Even if you don't want to eat the nettles yourself, give them to your chooks and you will find they will lay iron-rich eggs with beautiful orange yolks. Dried nettles also make excellent fodder for goats, horses and cattle.) Because of their astringent properties, nettles also make a fine cleansing agent, especially useful for people with oily skin or hair.

## Nettle Hair Conditioner

The presence of sulphur in nettles makes them good for skin, hair and nails. Use this recipe as a finishing rinse after shampooing, to stimulate hair growth and leave your hair shining and healthy.

*2 whole nettle plants (including roots)*
*5 cups (1.25 litres/40 fl oz) water*
*2½ tablespoons apple cider vinegar*

Simmer the nettles in water and vinegar in a non-aluminium saucepan for 1½–2 hours. Strain, cool and bottle the liquid, storing it in the refrigerator between uses.

Interestingly, the sting in the nettle plant is the result of formic acid, exactly the same stuff that ant stings are made of. In keeping with the paradoxes of botanical medicine, one finds an ointment made from nettle leaves is a soothing remedy for ant stings!

The juice of the common stinging nettle also contains a magic formula for those with high blood pressure. It is alkaline and a solvent for uric acid, so will help ward off rheumatism. Gypsy men planted nettles wherever they went, harvesting them for their medicinal properties, which probably accounted for the usual angst forthcoming from the local farmers!

*See also Asters*

## NEWSPAPERS

Given that almost half of our household waste is estimated to be paper-based products, manufactured from trees, it makes ecologically good sense to return this resource to the soil. Either shred the newspaper and cardboard and add them to your compost heap, or make *papier maché*, by soaking the sheets and squeezing them until almost dry, then arranging them in overlapping thicknesses around plants as a means of weed control. (As a bonus, newspapers return selenium to the soil. This trace element is thought to neutralise arsenic, the unhappy legacy of older-style insecticides often found in overworked soils.)

POTATOES, NOW, ARE A DIFFERENT THING,
THEY WANT TO GROW DOWN, THAT IS PLAIN,
BUT DON'T YE SEE, YOU MUST PLANT FOR THAT
WHEN THE MOON IS ON THE WANE.

FARMER BEN'S THEORY (19TH CENTURY AMERICAN ALMANAC)

## NUDITY

It is curious how often, in the old *herballs*, men and women were advised to sow seed when they were naked. 'The best husbandmen,' wrote one, 'would have the seedsman of turnips or rapes to be naked when he sows them.' Presumably, it was hoped that the gods might look more favourably upon the addled, nude gardener, than on a prosperously-clothed one. However, this advice was not always given for magical reasons. We should not sow when the ground is too cold for the seed and we are less likely to do this if we have to be naked at the same time.

## NURSE TREES

Certain trees can help regenerate spent soils, their dropped leaves helping to nourish the earth. One of these is the birch tree. Soil can actually be taken from around the base of an established birch tree and worked into another area, where plants are weak or diseased, helping them to recover. Old-time American farmers would drag a large brush made from birch branches over a freshly-ploughed field, in the belief that this treatment would optimise soil fertility. The poplar is another such 'nurse' tree, not only because it seems to encourage the growth of nearby grasses and wild flowers, but because, rather like eucalyptus trees, they are the first to reappear after a fire, thus helping to restore the scorched land to normal.

IF CUTTINGS ARE TAKEN FROM PLANTS WITH SHEARS, THEY WILL
NOT DO WELL. THEY MUST BE BROKEN OFF, SAYS THE OLD
WIVES' TALE, IN ORDER TO STRIKE SUCCESSFULLY.

# WISE OLD OAKS

The oak has been regarded as a sacred tree from earliest times and the magical acorn was enlisted by the Druids and ancient wise-women in spells and divination. (Did you know that the acorn-shaped bobbins on the end of cords used to pull blinds or curtains are a remnant of their use as a lucky charm in the home?) Be wary of felling an oak. Over time, it will send up shoots from the stump, forming a coppice, said to be haunted by Oakmen, who are understandably angry over the loss of their home. The poisonous fungi which grow on such stumps are said to be the fairies' attempt to harm passing mortals in revenge.

# O FOR AN ONION

*Onion skin very thin,*
*Mild winter coming in;*
*Onion skin very tough,*
*Winter coming cold and rough.*

If you can arrange for your onions to be planted close to beetroot or other members of the cabbage family, you may look forward to good crops of both. Onions and carrots are also good companions, as they repel each other's pests. Onions and peas, though, do not get on. Minced onion peelings, dug into the rose bed, will help keep the blooms bug-free. Alternatively, make up a spray of diluted onion juice and use it against red spider mites and aphids. Onions themselves are quite hardy but do suffer from infestations by thrips in certain circumstances. Interplanting onions with the 'plant doctor', chamomile, is thought to strengthen their resistance, too.

Here is a wonderful onion soup recipe, so thick you can almost stand your spoon up in your bowl. Onions, like garlic, are a potent natural antibiotic, containing allyl disulphate and cyclo alliin, natural antiseptic oils. Eat plenty of onions during the colder months and this will help to keep colds and 'flu at bay.

## Stick-To-Your-Ribs Onion Soup

*6 large Spanish onions*
*1 large leek*
*50 g (1½ oz) butter*
*30 g (1 oz) flour*
*2 tablespoons breadcrumbs*
*110 g (3½ oz) lean ham, diced*
*freshly ground pepper and salt*
*300 ml (10 fl oz) milk*

*3 large potatoes, peeled*
*1 carrot, peeled and sliced*
*thick cream*
*chopped shallots*

Peel the onions and leek, slice thinly and brown in the butter. Add the flour and breadcrumbs, then the ham and seasonings and then the milk, a little at a time, stirring in well. Cook over a low heat for 30 minutes. Meanwhile, place the potatoes and carrots in water and bring them to the boil. Cook until tender, then cool and mash them, with a little extra milk and butter, until creamy. Add to the onion mixture and thin the soup to a desired consistency with the cream. Garnish with natural yoghurt, chives and a dusting of paprika.

*See also Beans; Carrots; Cuts And Grazes; Mosquitoes; Potatoes; Romantic Roses; Tomatoes*

## PANSIES

Pansies are very fortunate indeed in a garden. Country folk say the larger petal represents the happy mother, the smaller ones her brood of loyal children. Pansies are equally favoured by the fairies. (It was 'the little Western flower', used with such devastating effect by Oberon, in a love potion in *A Midsummer Night's Dream*.)

## PARSLEY

Herbalists of old were aware of the digestive properties of parsley. Gypsies maintained that if (and only if) you sowed parsley on Good Friday, health and happiness would be yours in the coming year. Parsley brings fortune and fertility to a household and is popularly credited with causing pregnancy. Country folk say, 'To sow parsley is to sow babies.'

Parsley should not be given from one person to another, nor bought. Neither should it be dug up or transplanted in the garden, lest the devil plant noxious weeds in the original spot. The safest method is to indicate the whereabouts of the parsley patch and let people help themselves. This tradition may have something to do with the Greek custom of lining coffins with parsley, for it would have been unlucky to meddle with graves.

A few parsley plants are never enough in a garden, in my opinion. Plant parsley by carrots, to repel carrot fly, and near asparagus, roses and tomatoes, to deter aphids and attract ladybirds. As well as its protective role, parsley adds strength and flavour to fruit and vegetables. Add to all these uses its importance in cooking (as a garnish or tea) and in beauty care (as an astringent or a conditioner) and you have plenty of reasons for planting parsley. Keep it away from mint, though.

Parsley seeds are slow to germinate and many superstitions have arisen because of this. One very old belief has it that the seeds have to travel right to the centre of the earth, to visit the devil, and then come back, before the plants will appear. Another old wives' tale says pouring boiling water over newly-set parsley seed will hasten the process of germination — presumably by fooling the parsley into believing it has already visited the Other Place ...

*See also Asparagus; Chives; Preserving Flowers And Plants; Romantic Roses; Skin Care; Tomatoes; Parsnips*

REMEMBER ON ST VINCENT'S DAY (JANUARY 22)
IF THAT THE SUN HIS BEAMS DO DISPLAY
BE SURE TO TAKE HIS TRANSIENT BEAM
WHICH THROUGH THE CASEMENTS SHEDS A GLEAM,
FOR 'TIS A TOKEN BRIGHT AND CLEAR
OF PROSPEROUS WEATHER ALL THE YEAR.

(PROVERB)

## PATHS

A garden of aromatic flowers and leaves is indeed a delight. Let's start with scent underfoot and create aromatic paths which don't necessarily *go* anywhere, except possibly to a nook beneath a shady, fragrant tree.

Old bricks, placed on their sides, make a distinctive path. Gaps of about 5 cm (2 in) square should be left here and there, where aromatic herbs of a carpeting habit can be planted. Stone pavers, shingle and gravel also look most attractive.

Sir Francis Bacon wrote in 1625 of:

> *... wild thyme and water mint (as) perfuming the aire most delightfulle, being trodden upon and crushed ...*

Heed his tip and plant a number of the different varieties of aromatic herbs in your path. Set plantlets about 1 m (3⅓ ft) from each other. They will soon spread to cover half a metre (yard) square, or more. Among the best choices are the prostrate thymes, especially *Thymus serpyllum* 'Coccineus', a mat of dark green dotted with dozens of tiny red flowers. 'Pink Chintz', with its salmon-coloured flowers, is also very pretty, as is the well-loved basil thyme, which bears purple flowers and releases a warm, minty fragrance when walked upon. Corsican savory bears tiny spikes of pure white in summer, and also releases a delicious scent underfoot.

Most herbs enjoy dry conditions but, if planting mint, remember it likes moisture. A little well-rotted manure, tucked around the roots at planting times, will not go astray, either. Complement it with the dwarf chamomile *Anthemis nobilis* 'Treneague', which releases a refreshing apple-like scent every time it is trodden upon. Indeed, in Spain, it is commonly known as *manzanilla*, or 'little apple'.

*See also Strawberries*

## PEPPER

If you're having trouble with various bugs attacking young seedlings, try sprinkling pepper along the drill with the seed. If you listen closely, perhaps you'll hear the bugs sneezing! Similarly, pepper dusted over dew-wet leaves will repel caterpillars.

*See also Ants*

IF NEW YEAR'S EVE NIGHT, WIND BLOWETH SOUTH
IT BETOKENETH WARMTH AND GROWTH;
IF WEST, MUCH MILK AND FISH IN THE SEA;
IF NORTH, MUCH COLD AND STORMS THERE'LL BE;
IF EAST, THE TREES WILL BEAR FRUIT;
IF NORTH-EAST, FLEE IT, MAN AND BRUTE.

## PERIWINKLES

Soft, blue periwinkles, although very pretty, would probably only bring sorrow to a household, according to superstition. They are said to have been bound in wreaths worn by condemned criminals, and to flourish on graves, making them an ominous choice in a garden.

## PILLOWS

Sometimes the greatest gifts are a good night's sleep and being able to breathe sweet, fragrant air. If you're clever with a needle and thread, you can make old-fashioned sleepy-pillows. Here is a charming herbal combination to fill them:

*2 tablespoons each rose buds, rose
leaves and rosemary
a cotton ball dipped in
bergamot oil, neroli oil and
gardenia oil in turn*

The Romans were the first to add dried rose petals to pillows, while Queen Elizabeth I's mattress was said to have been padded with 'lady's bedstraw' (*Galium odorata*). George III could not sleep without his favourite hop pillow and Victorian ladies delighted in lavender cushions, turning their faces towards the refreshing scent to avert attacks of the vapours. Fragrant, flower-filled pillows delicately scent the bedroom, calm jangled nerves and soothe fractious babies. For best results, make them in natural fabrics, such as cotton, muslin and linen. The weave allows the perfumes through by letting the flowers 'breathe'.

*See also Drawer Pillows; Hops; Sachets*

## PIMPLES

Daisies and cucumber are both herbs for beauty care. In days of old, gypsy girls would use both to clear blemishes from their skin. Today, you can use your blender to extract the juices, then mix them with lemon juice and witch hazel. If necessary, dilute the mixture with pure, boiled water, for a refreshing, astringent skin lotion.

PATIENCE IS A FLOWER THAT GROWS
NOT IN EVERY MAN'S GARDEN.

(PROVERB)

## PLANT RELATIONSHIPS

There has long beeen conjecture about relationships between plants. Louisiana gardeners say that to destroy one plant in the garden causes all others of the same species nearby to pine. To test this theory, J. Rodale, the organic gardening authority, grew slips from two coleus plants, then burnt and buried the remains of one parent plant. Although they did not die, the slips from the burned coleus grew markedly less well than those from the surviving parent.

A tree always does best near a friend. A few years ago, I was given a rather rare golden-spored fern, but it made little progress until I remembered that plants like to be with their own kind. I replanted it near a maidenhair and it is still doing well. Similarly, if you take plants when you move to a new home, be sure to place them near each other. They will be happier closer to old friends.

Empathy between plant and owner is also strong. A friend

described the effect of one illness upon two houseplants. When she took the plants into hospital, she found they collapsed on her return from the operating theatre. The sceptical might suggest that neglect from a nurse created the dramatic prostration. However, the understanding between plants and people suggests that the collapse was sympathetic rather than coincidental.

## POO

If you've ever wondered about the origin of the phrase 'burying the Chinaman', I am reliably told that it dates from the times when Chinese migrants took the jobs of carting the 'night-soil' trucks around to homes which had not yet been connected to the sewer system here in Sydney. Gossip had it that they used this night-soil as fertiliser for their vegetables, accounting for their wondrous size and healthy appearance. Don't be too quick to pooh-pooh (sorry!) this idea. In these ecologically-aware times, I know several people who swear by the (diluted) contents of their chamber pot for fertiliser.

*See also Dogs*

## POSSUMS

If you are at your wit's end with possums feasting on the tender new shoots of your roses, try smearing new foliage with soft soap (available from chemists) dissolved in a little water, with bitter aloes or white pepper mixed in to make a paste. This will involve patience and persistence, but it is extremely effective.

I AM JUST COME OUT OF THE GARDEN ON THE MOST ORIENTAL OF ALL EVENINGS, AND FROM BREATHING ODOURS BEYOND THOSE OF ARABY. THE ACACIAS, WHICH THE ARABIANS HAVE THE SENSE TO WORSHIP, ARE COVERED WITH BLOSSOMS, THE HONEYSUCKLES DANGLE FROM EVERY TREE IN FESTOONS, THE SERINGEAS ARE THICKETS OF SWEETS, AND THE NEW CUT HAY IN THE FIELD TEMPERS THE BALMY GALES WITH SIMPLE FRESHNESS.

HORACE WALPOLE, ELEVEN AT NIGHT (JUNE 19, 1795)

# POTATOES

Comfrey is rich in potassium, nitrogen and phosphates, making it an excellent plant fertiliser. For a really bumper, well-flavoured crop of potatoes that keep better and longer than average, place comfrey leaves in the trenches before planting.

Potatoes do well planted with beans, peas, cabbage and sweet corn. Try setting one row of potatoes to two of peas, with a horseradish plant at either end, for optimum results. However, there are many plants which do not get on with potatoes. Sunflowers stunt their growth and pumpkin, cucumbers, raspberries and squash are all bad for potatoes. Gardeners should take particular care to place onions and potatoes, noted enemies, at opposite ends of the garden. Old-time gardeners in the American Ozarks say that 'onions make the 'taters cry their eyes out'. Scatter bran amongst your potato crop to beat hungry potato beetles. They gorge themselves on the bran and are then sluggish enough to be murdered easily. Alternatively, set eggplant around the potato patch to act as a trap crop (an attractive lure to the pests). When harvested, don't store apples near your potatoes as they will give the potatoes a sour flavour and affect their keeping ability.

*See also Beans; Bruises; Skin Care; Tomatoes*

# POTPOURRI

Askham's *Herball* (1520) said:

*Drye roses putte to the nose to smel do comforte the Brayne and the Herte ...*

This is still so true today. Floral potpourris scent the air and make life wonderfully fragrant. Choose flowers for their scent and colour (such as all kinds of roses, lavender, carnations, lily of the valley, violets, wallflowers and honeysuckle) or just for their colour (such as candytuft, cornflowers, marigolds, hydrangeas, pansies, nasturtiums and zinnias). Place a handful of potpourri in a mill, grind it to a fine powder and tie into small bags as gifts. I like this recipe for a sweet-and-sour style potpourri:

> *½ teaspoon sandalwood oil*
> *1 tablespoon raw sugar*
> *¼ teaspoon each allspice,*
> *cinnamon, nutmeg and cloves*
> *50 g (1½ oz) dried red rose petals*
> *15 g (½ oz) jasmine buds*

Mix the oil with the sugar and spices and sprinkle over the dried flower petals. Cover the mixture for 3 weeks and then display in an open jar.

'No bought potpourri is so pleasant as that made from one's own garden, for the petals of the flowers one has gathered at home hold the sunshine and memories of summer, and of past summers only the sunny days should be remembered ...' So wrote Eleanour Sinclair Rohde in *The Scented Garden* (1920). With the obvious exception of roses, I can think of no more delightful contribution to potpourri than scented geraniums. So easily grown inside or outside the house, they give a joyful show of ornamental foliage and bright flowers

throughout the year. Here is a delightful old 'receipt' for a scented geranium potpourri:

To one pinte of lightly pressed rose petals and halfe a pinte of scented leaved geraniums, add half a pinte of lavender flowers or one eighth of an ounce of lavender oyle. When the flowers are dry and crisp, add one quarter of a teaspoon of cinnamon, mace and powdered cloves; two to three teaspoons of orris root and one eighth of a teaspoon oyle of geranium.

Mix these ingredients well and store them in an airtight container for 2 or 3 weeks. Mix them well again before use.

'I have never known anyone not to be delighted with the delicious smell of leaves, which they retain long after they are dried ...' wrote Mrs Earle in *Potpourri from a Scented Garden* (1905). Herbs and leaves play as important a role in making a fragrant potpourri as flowers do. Some are used for their attractive appearance (such as Japanese cherry leaves or lime blossom bracts) but mostly they are used for their aroma. Lavender, eucalyptus, lemon verbena, rosemary, thyme and sweet woodruff all become more fragrant when dried.

The roots, berries, seeds or even fruits of various species are sometimes added to potpourri to give a more full-bodied scent. Spices often have considerable fixing properties, as well as great subtlety of aroma. The ones most commonly used in potpourri are the sweet spices—anise, cinnamon, cloves, nutmeg, vanilla or allspice. To give a faintly oriental scent, try using cardamom or coriander instead.

*See also Geraniums; Sachets*

## PRAYERFUL PLANTS

Prayer for plants is an ancient concept. The Tudors favoured a formula given by Leonard Mascall in *The Booke of the Arte and Manner Howe to Plante and Graffe* (1572):

*And whensoever ye shall plante or graffe, it shall be mete and good for you to saye as followeth — in the Name of God the Father, the Sonne and the Holy Ghoste, Amen. Increase and multiply, and replenish the earth in thy Name, O Lorde, we set, plant and graffe, desiring that by thy mighty power they may encrease and multiply upon the earth ...*

The Rev. Franklin Loehr, author of *The Power of Prayer Upon Plants*, says that if cursing works (as Christ was said to have cursed the barren fig tree, in Mark II 13:21), so will prayer. He conducted a series of experiments where participants prayed over a jug of water which was then poured over planted seeds of corn, lima beans and sweet peas, while a control group received untreated water. He found that both the corn and lima beans receiving 'prayer water' germinated first, while the sweet peas out-flowered their control cousins three to one.

Much of this research into plant sensitivity, which throws new light on a whole range of ancient folk beliefs, was roused by the work of Clive Backster, an expert in polygraphy and lie-detection. One evening, he lightheartedly attached the leaves of a *Dracaeana* to a polygraph machine and found that the plant exhibited mild emotional stimulation when watered. Further experiments followed, the most noteworthy being when Backster threatened to burn a leaf and the polygraph tracing leapt dramatically in a 'fear' reaction.

*See also Holy Plants*

THE RABBIT HAS A CHARMING FACE
BUT ITS PRIVATE LIFE IS A DISGRACE,
I REALLY DARE NOT NAME TO YOU
THE DREADFUL THINGS THAT RABBITS DO.

# PRESERVING FLOWERS AND PLANTS

Don't just confine your garden's harvest to items for food or household use. Indulge your sense of beauty, too, by preserving the glorious colours of autumn leaves.

Cut a selection of short branches from different shrubs and trees you admire. The trick is to cut the branches just *before* the leaves start to turn. Pound the cut ends of the branches with the blunt ends of your secateurs. Make up a solution of 1 part glycerine to 2 parts very hot water, pour it into a wide-mouthed jar and stand the branches in the solution. Leave them for at least 2 weeks. During this time the leaves will have absorbed the solution and will actually feel pliable instead of crisp. They should last for several years and make a wonderful addition to both fresh and dried flower arrangements.

Similarly, why not try your hand at preserving bright spring and summer flowers, like roses, zinnias, crocus and narcissi, via the old-fashioned sandbox method. This is usually successful for even quite delicate flowers like violets and snowdrops. Fill a shoebox

with about 2.5 cm (1 in) of very fine sand (pet shops sell cleaned aquarium sand, for fish tanks, which is ideal). Select your flowers, being sure to leave at least 1.5 cm (½ in) of stem, and 'plant' the flowers upright in the sand so that they do not touch each other. Gently sift more sand, or a one to one mixture of sand and borax (this is quicker but be careful—borax is toxic) over the flowers and leave for at least a month in a sunny, dry spot. By this time, the flowers should be crisp and may be used to decorate wreaths, for potpourri or for other crafty ideas.

*See also Bookmarks; Violets*

## PRESERVING PARSLEY

To store parsley for use year-round (and I *never* seem to have enough), pick and tie bunches of the fresh herb and drop them into 4 litres (128 fl oz) of rapidly boiling water, to which 2 tablespoons of salt and the juice of 1 lemon have been added. Cook the parsley for no more than 3 minutes. Pick out the bunches with tongs, drain them on absorbent paper and then dry them very quickly in a warm oven. Store the crisp parsley in airtight jars. When needed for cookery, dip a bunch in tepid water for a minute or two.

## PRESERVING LEMONS

When buying or picking lemons, remember that they do not ripen off the tree. Select only those that are firm, bright and heavy for their size. As a general rule, a deep yellow colour indicates more juice, while greenish fruit is usually more acid and less juicy. (The latter is the better choice when a higher acid content is required for a recipe, such as tenderising meat.)

If you have a glut from a particularly heavy home harvest, refrigerate or freeze the juice.

**TIP: when freezing lemon juice, refrigerate the lemons for several hours before squeezing. Remove any seeds and make sure none of the oil from the skin of the lemon gets into the tray or ice cube container, as this will make the juice bitter.**

Alternatively you can home store the lemons, using this method:

Line a wooden case or cardboard carton with newspaper and spread a thin layer of sand on the base. Pack a layer of lemons over this, spaced so they are not touching each other (touching may cause discolouration over time). Cover this layer with sand and continue until all the lemons are packed away. This actually seems to improve the juice content of the fruit.

An even quicker idea—although it may look rather peculiar—is to use the legs of old pantyhose. Simply pop in a lemon, then tie a knot, pop in another lemon and so on. This means they do not touch each other and have plenty of fresh air circulating around them, thus maximising their storage life. This is also very good for all other citrus, especially grapefruit and limes, which can be stored, hung up, for at least 6–8 weeks this way without going mouldy.

# PUMPKIN PATCH

Pumpkins are one of the very ancient vegetables of the world, dating from 7000 BC in Central America. Beautiful pumpkin-shaped pottery vessels, found in pre-Incan burial sites, indicate the abundance of varieties known to the ancient Indians there.

The name 'pumpkin' comes from the Greek *sikvos pepon*, which means 'cooked in the sun'. They are possibly the most popular of their clan, containing more nourishment than their cousins, the marrows or squashes. Even pumpkin sprouts are particularly rich in protein and essential fatty acids. Grown like bean sprouts, they will be ready for eating in less than a week.

Pumpkin's flavour and texture enhance both savoury and sweet dishes. Don't just limit yourself to using the pulp in soups. Use pumpkin in casseroles, chutneys, soufflés and pies. The purée may be mixed with other ingredients to form delicious puddings, or serve it hot with butter, cream and candied ginger, as a dessert in its own right. Pumpkins make a mouthwatering spiced preserve. They can also be served as a vegetable side-dish or laced with brandy, breadcrumbs and grated cheese and used as a stuffing for pork.

## Pumpkin and Pecan Scones

*1 or 2 eggs*
*⅓ cup (80 g/2½ oz) sugar*
*15 ml (½ fl oz) maple syrup*
*1 cup (250 g/8 oz) cold, mashed pumpkin*
*1 teaspoon melted butter*
*¾ cup (180 ml/6 fl oz) cream*
*2 cups (250 g/8 oz) self-raising flour*
*½ teaspoon ground cinnamon*
*½ cup (60 g/2 oz) toasted pecans, finely chopped*
*1 teaspoon each grated candied lemon and orange peel*

Beat the eggs and the sugar together until thick, add the maple syrup and the pumpkin. Add the melted butter to the cream. Sift the flour into a basin, fold in the egg mixture, then the cream, then the pecans. Mix to a soft dough and knead once, lightly, on a well-floured surface. Roll out to approximately 1¼ cm (½ in) thickness and cut into squares. Place the scones on a buttered baking sheet, brush them with a little milk and bake them in a hot oven for 10–15 minutes, or until done.

Pumpkins are extremely (some would say riotously!) easy to grow in any suburban garden. Ideally they should have plenty of room to ramble but, even if you haven't much space, they can be trained along a fence or over a (very) strong trellis. Red-Indian-style tripods are easy to make by tying three 2½ m (8 ft) poles together at the top, like a wigwam, and planting one seedling against each pole. As the plants grow, make sure you tie them loosely to the poles with heavy twine, as they won't cling by themselves. You can also try growing pumpkins with corn, as they make excellent companions for each other. For a space-saving garden, plant corn in concentric circles, with beans and pumpkins in between.

Pumpkins are fairly hardy but slugs like them and tend to lurk in the mulch around the vine. Pumpkin beetles (the little, yellow ladybird lookalikes) can be a nuisance, but are easily controlled with derris dust. Pumpkins are also susceptible to powdery mildew, a fungus which actually prefers dry conditions, so cure it by keeping water up to the plant.

Harvest your pumpkins in autumn, when the fruit is fully ripe, the skin has started to harden and the vine has begun to die back. Cure them for at least 2 weeks in the sun, to complete the ripening process. If you are planning to store them, make sure you leave a stem length of 10–15 cm (4–6 in) and keep them in a dry place. Traditionally, pumpkins were stored in straw or hung in mesh bags, thus allowing air to circulate about them. Check every week for mould and, if you see any starting to develop, wipe it off straight away with an oily cloth.

> **TIP:** Having harvested the pumpkin, there are few cooks who haven't found the prospect of carving it rather daunting. The easiest way is to pretend it's an orange. First, slice it straight across the stem end, then across the bottom, so the thing will sit upright. Then, following the curve of the fruit, slide a thin sharp knife under the skin and peel it from top to bottom. Now cut it in half, scoop out the strings and reserve the seeds, then steam, boil or bake it, according to the recipe you are following.

Even simpler is to cut the unpeeled pumpkin in half, scoop out the seeds and strings and place the halves in a well-buttered pan, shell sides up. Bake it in a medium oven for about 1 hour, or until the shell starts to fall in. Allow the halves to cool before scooping out the pulp and processing it as a purée or filling.

*See also Battered Blossoms; Marrows; Potatoes*

IF CLOUDS BE BRIGHT, 'TWILL CLEAR TONIGHT;
IF CLOUDS BE DARK, 'TWILL RAIN, D'YOU HARK?

## RABBITS

Even if they're not partial to your crops, rabbits can ruin a garden by digging up the soil and disturbing the roots. Planting onions, spearmint or chives will keep bunnies at bay; nor do they like the smell of rosemary, box or nicotiana. Otherwise you can sprinkle the ground with powdered ashes and cayenne pepper. Scattering a few mint leaves around barns storing grains like rice and oats will also keep rabbits away.

IF THE COCK MOULT BEFORE THE HEN
WE SHALL HAVE WEATHER THICK AND THIN.
IF THE HEN MOULT BEFORE THE COCK
WE SHALL HAVE WEATHER HARD AS A ROCK.

## RADISHES

Radishes grow well with cucumbers, squash and melons, and will repel cucumber beetle and red spider mites. They also grow well near peas and chervil but will suffer if hyssop is nearby. If you want them to be especially tender, set lettuce amongst them in summer.

*See also Hyssop; Lettuce*

## RED FLOWERS

The generous seed pod of the scarlet poppy was said to bring many children. Bright geraniums, marigolds and nasturtiums are lucky, as are most red and yellow flowers. Medieval 'wise women' used all sorts of red and yellow flowers in charms against evil—red symbolising life, and yellow, the smiling sun.

## ROMANTIC ROSES

Of one of the most celebrated flowers in the world, it was Walter de la Mare who wrote:

*Oh, no one knows*
*Through what wild centuries*
*Roves back the Rose.*

The rose is the oldest domesticated flower on record. Fossil remains of the rose, said to be at least 35 million years old, have been found. A rose is more than a beautiful flower. It has symbolised love, passion, purity, war and peace, as well as having been used as food, drink and medicine.

When planting a new rose, put a clove of garlic underneath it. The roots will take up the essence of the garlic and help repel aphids. Interestingly, commercial perfumers interplant roses with garlic because it results in a stronger, sweeter perfume. Parsley and onions are also helpful and mignonette lettuce or a carpet of low-growing purslane will improve the moisture content of the soil. Don't plant roses with any other plants which have woody, outspread roots as they will compete for the same area.

Harvest your roses to prepare soothing, scented cosmetics, delicate jams, jellies and syrups, butters and ices and romantic

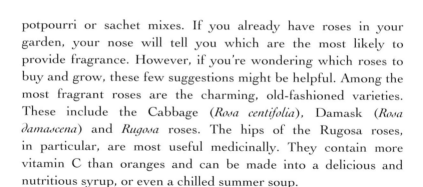

potpourri or sachet mixes. If you already have roses in your garden, your nose will tell you which are the most likely to provide fragrance. However, if you're wondering which roses to buy and grow, these few suggestions might be helpful. Among the most fragrant roses are the charming, old-fashioned varieties. These include the Cabbage (*Rosa centifolia*), Damask (*Rosa damascena*) and *Rugosa* roses. The hips of the Rugosa roses, in particular, are most useful medicinally. They contain more vitamin C than oranges and can be made into a delicious and nutritious syrup, or even a chilled summer soup.

## Rose Hip Jelly

*500 g (17 oz) rose hips*
*lemon juice*
*water*
*sugar*

Place the hips in a large, non-aluminium saucepan with enough cold water to cover. Bring them to the boil, reduce the heat and simmer until the hips are soft. Mash the hips with a wooden spoon or spatula. Place the pulp in a muslin jelly-bag and allow it to strain overnight. In the morning, press down well on the hips to extract all the juice. Measure the juice, and for each 600 ml (20 fl oz), add 350 g (11½ oz) sugar and the juice of one lemon. Return the mixture to the pan and bring it to the boil. Continue to cook until the mixture begins to gel, then spoon it into heated, sterile jars and cap securely.

## ROSEMARY FOR REMEMBRANCE

The Arabs prized rosemary highly, clipping it into low hedges as a protective border for their rose beds. English monks continued this tradition, planting rosemary as a specific barrier against illness. It should be allowed to grow near all entrances to a house, for it will also foil thieves. If they step on it, it is said that they instantly lose their inclination to steal.

*See also Body Oil; Body Powders; Fertilisers; Flowers As Food;*
*Freshening The House; Garlic; Geraniums; Holy Plants; O For An Onion;*
*Parsley; Potpourri; Tansy; Tomatoes; Vinegars; Violets*

> WHEN FISH REFUSE BAIT OR FLY,
> STORM IT IS THAT NOW IS NIGH.

## RUE THE THOUGHT

Rue is a risky herb, often blamed for bringing sorrow to a household. It is best planted far away from the house, and preferably in hallowed ground. Aristotle was one of the few proponents of rue, assuring us that fresh branches hung from kitchen rafters 'dispelled scorpions and serpents from dwellings'.

> THERE ARE FAIRIES AT THE BOTTOM OF OUR GARDEN,
> IT'S NOT SO VERY, VERY FAR AWAY.
> YOU PASS THE GARDENER'S SHED
> AND YOU JUST KEEP STRAIGHT AHEAD.
> I DO SO HOPE THEY'VE REALLY COME TO STAY!
>
> ROSE FYLEMAN, C. 1900

## SACHETS

Make five-petalled flowers, perhaps roses, out of organdy or any other pretty and fairly thin (but non-porous) cloth. Each petal should be made double, like a tiny pouch, filled with dried rose petals or a potpourri mixture. Sew the petals together at the base to form a flower and then add a couple of artificial leaves and pearl beads in the centre. These pretty corsages from your garden are not only good money-raisers for fêtes, but will also make charming gifts and place-markers at parties.

Don't neglect the menfolk in your household. Whether or not they will admit it, they, too, like a bit of fragrance. Fill that wardrobe of dreary suits with a breath of fresh air by making sachets containing one of these blends:

- Equal parts of pine and lavender.
- Lemon verbena, mint and lavender.
- Nutmeg, lemon verbena and geranium (nutmeg-scented, for preference).

*See also Bath Sachets; Drawer Pillows; Moth Deterrents; Pillows*

## SAGE ADVICE

Sage is considered very lucky, although superstitions concerning it are contradictory. The English would hang a sprig over the front door when a member of the family went on holidays and, for as long as it did not droop or spoil, the person was happy and safe. The French, however, say the flowers should always be picked off, for if they are allowed to bloom,

misfortune will befall the family. Another European superstition says that if sage grows profusely in a garden, it is a sure sign that the wife rules the roost.

Gather and eat sage regularly if you wish to enjoy a long and happy life, for:

> *He that would live for aye*
> *Must eat sage in May.*

As it also improves eyesight and sharpens the memory, it is a wise staple in a home herb garden. Old wives would often scold 'How can a man die who has sage in his garden?'

Our ancestors brewed sage for use as a tea and used the leaves to cleanse the teeth and strengthen the gums. Sage's pungent flavour marries well with certain foods, especially rich cheeses, game or strong-flavoured meats and sausages. It is also a good moth deterrent. With its vibrant flavour, sage is useful as an antiseptic and as a freshening gargle. A strong tea made from sage, regularly combed through the hair, will effectively darken greying strands.

*See also Cabbages; Tubs; Window Boxes*

## SCENTED GERANIUMS

The Victorians used scented geraniums whenever possible, planting them in protected, walled gardens and glassed-in conservatories, or bringing them into the house, where the brushing of the leaves with wide Victorian crinolines would create a delicious fragrance for passers-by. A favourite setting for potted varieties of these plants was up the sides of staircases, where their scent would readily fill the air. These pretty ornamentals are quite happy in either sun or partial shade and require only occasional watering if they've been well-potted.

Perhaps the most famous is *Pelargonium capitatum*. Its essence was widely used to replace the more expensive attar of roses in perfume manufacturing. Those who prefer spicy scents will want *Pelargonium crispum* 'Variegatum' close by, with its curly leaves that carry the scent of verbena. More exotic varieties include *Pelargonium tomentosum* — its leaves and stems can be cooked and used to make a mint-flavoured jelly — and the oak-leaved geranium, *Pelargonium quercifolium* 'Major', which smells a little like incense and is the perfect plant for scenting a warm room on a dark winter's evening.
*See also Bookmarks; Potpourri; Vinegars*

## SEEDLINGS

To ensure seedlings grow tall and strong, it is advised that you do as the Ceylonese did when planting tea — leap high into the air to demonstrate the result that is required!
*See also Cutworms; Gifts From Your Garden*

IF THE THUNDER COMES FROM THE NORTH, IT WILL SURELY
DOUBLE IN WRATH;
IF IT COMES FROM THE SOUTH, IT WILL OPEN ITS MOUTH;
IF IT COMES FROM THE WEST, IT WILL NEVER BE AT REST;
IF IT COMES FROM THE EAST, IT WILL NEVER GIVE US PEACE.

(CORNISH PROVERB)

# SEEDS AND STRIKING CUTTINGS

To make hard-coated seeds germinate faster, pour boiling water over them before planting. This will not harm the seeds; it only softens the shell.

If you're trying to strike a cutting from a woody-stemmed plant, such as a lilac or hydrangea, slit the stem end and tuck a grain of wheat inside. The more rapid germination of the grain will encourage the cutting to root more quickly.

*See also Surprise Packets*

# SKIN CARE

Do you have sensitive skin? Watch out for the following plants, then, for they all have a high likelihood of causing dermatitis, rashes, redness and intense itching: parsley, parsnips, primroses, rhus trees, okra, asparagus and potatoes (the plants, not the roots) and chrysanthemums. Certain grasses and weeds, notably onion weeds, produce sap which has an irritant effect upon the skin. Oddly enough, men seem more susceptible than women. Pants, a long-sleeved shirt that fits snugly at the wrists, and gloves should all be worn. If a rash does develop, cleanse the area with a mild, unscented soap and tepid water, then apply a soothing cream.

A quick and easy alternative for soothing rashes is to grind up one or two aspirin tablets with water, to make a paste, and smooth it onto the affected area. This has a remarkable ability to dull any pain and reduce inflammation. Wheatgerm oil, vitamin E oil and propolis oil (a powerful natural

antibiotic with fungicidal properties manufactured by bees, available from your health food shop), are all worth keeping in your first aid cabinet. All are very good at soothing skin rashes in the sensitive gardener. Another product from health food shops (a boon for anyone susceptible to environmental irritants) is spirulina, a sea vegetable sold in powdered or tablet form. It contains phenylalanine, a natural amino acid which helps the body suppress allergic symptoms, especially wheezing or runny eyes.

*See also Aloe Vera; Bath Sachets; Body Oil; Body Powders; Foot Care; Hands; Lavender; Lemony Loveliness; Sunburn*

OF COURSE THE MINUTE I SHOWED INTEREST IN GARDENING, I RAN INTO THE GARDEN-CLUB-LATIN-NAMERS. 'GOSH, WHAT PRETTY RED NASTURTIUMS,' I SAID.

'OH, YOU MUST MEAN MY *TROPAELEÜM MAJUS*,' THE LATIN-NAMER ANSWERED WITH A CONDESCENDING LITTLE LAUGH.

THE SECRET THING I HAVE FOUND OUT ABOUT THE LATIN-NAMERS IS THAT VERY FEW OF THEM HAVE GARDENS. 'TOO BUSY WITH MY GARDEN CLUBS,' ONE TOLD ME LAST SPRING WHEN SHE CAME UP TO BORROW SOME FLOWERS FOR THEIR MEETING.

BETTY MACDONALD, *ONIONS IN THE STEW*, (HAMMOND, HAMMOND & CO., GREAT BRITAIN)

## SLUGS

Being strongly aromatic, aniseed plants seem immune to most garden pests. In particular, snails and slugs seem to give it a very wide berth, so it will help protect other plants growing nearby. Other methods include spreading sharp grit, lime or broken eggshells around plants, or making a gutter of salt. Slugs and snails would both hate to cross any of these barriers. Salt, incidentally, is very useful in the garden as a weed killer and pesticide as well. I remember my grandmother grimly tipping salt directly onto slugs and snail, when I was a child, dissolving them into a putrid (but oh-so-satisfying) frothy, green slime. Sheets of wet newspaper left on the grass overnight will attract snails and slugs, too—you'll be amazed how many. Pick them off in the morning and drop them into a bucket of heavily-salted water.

If you have chooks or ducks, let them have a run in the vegetable patch for they consider slugs and snails a delicacy. Orange-peel (or grapefruit-peel) halves are potent slug attractants. Place the peel cups upside-down in the garden overnight. You will be surprised, next morning, to count the number of slugs which have wriggled underneath.

A medieval herbalist, Richard Bradley, described the use of horsehair ropes in the garden to deter slugs and snails. He recommended that they be tied or wrapped about the stems of susceptible plants. He seems to have loathed slugs and snails as much as I do, for he smugly comments that the horsehair being '... so full of stubs and straggling Pointes, no slug or snail can pass over them without wounding themselves to Death'.

*See also Lavender; Nettles; Pumpkin Patch*

## SNAILS

A morning tour of the garden after a rainy night can make hand-picking of snails a lengthy process, but an extremely satisfying one. My old neighbour used to fling them—with some malice—onto the road, then listen to them getting crushed by cars. They love a tipple (and will drown in the process), so leaving saucers of beer or even empty beer cans out at night will make for easy collection. They won't cross a thick line of ash or hydrated lime either, so this makes an effective barrier for precious cabbage or lettuce heads.

*See also Nettles*

## SNAKES

In a tropical climate
or remote area, snakes
can present a real problem
for the gardener. Even if
you do not live in such a
place, there is always a chance,
no matter how slim, that you might
disturb a snake or spider while you
are gardening, particularly if you are in
an old garden that has not been cared for
for some time. *Always* wear sturdy gloves and, if
you do get bitten, forget about first aid and go straight to the
hospital outpatients' ward. Applying ice only causes a chill and a
tourniquet—although it always seemed to work for the Lone
Ranger—is more likely to just cut off your circulation. In short,
don't waste time. Seek expert help as soon as possible. (If you are
not near a hospital, bandage over the bite and up the limb, as
though for a sprain, and keep as still as possible until you can get
medical help.)

## SOAP

In grandma's day, dishwashing was done in a large pot or dish
and the soapy water was thrown over the flower bed by the back
door. Soapy water is still an excellent means of getting rid of
aphids and also helps to repel flies. Be certain to use soap, though,
*not* detergent.

## SPELLS

If you are determined to meet the fairies at the bottom of your garden (and I have always longed to), you must plant wild thyme and marigolds. The wild thyme should 'be gathered near the side of a hill where fayries used to be oft, and the grass of a fayrie throne'. Like other flowers that are fairy favourites, wild thyme is dangerous to bring into a house. Primroses also boast a unique power. They make the invisible visible and to eat them is a sure way to see the fairies. If you touch a fairy rock with the correct number of primroses in a posy, the way is opened to Fairyland and all its treasures, but the wrong number opens the door to doom.

An old charm to 'see the fairies' advises you to 'wash all the toppes of wild thyme and marigold flowers with sallet oyle and rosewatter', steep the liquid for several days, then drink it. The best place to sit while doing this is near (never in) a fairy ring of mushrooms. These circles of yellow or white flowers, or more often mushrooms, spring up where the fairies dance, or above their underground cities. If one appears on your lawn, walk around it carefully nine times in the direction of the sun and you may be able to hear the fairies talking and laughing (if not the neighbours ...). Do not press the issue if you cannot hear them, though, as they are terribly shy. Remember, you are very privileged they are there, for, as Spenser wrote: 'Whoever lives in a house built by a fairy ring shall wondrously prosper.'

To make that special wish come true, jump into the centre of the ring with your eyes shut, wish hard, and then jump quickly out again.

*See also Clover; Fairy Flora;*

## SPIRITUAL GARDENING

Louisiana gardeners say that whenever you give a cutting of a plant 'with a good heart', it will grow well. For complete success, cuttings should always be struck in threes and planted in threes, too. Perhaps this is in recollection of the importance of the Holy Trinity.

*See also Holy Plants*

## SCENTED STATIONERY

Don't just line the shelves of the linen press with scented paper. It is so easy to perfume writing paper and handkerchiefs by storing them with bags of dry potpourri mixture. Scented notepaper can be kept for your own use and also makes a pretty present. Buy a box of flower-decorated notelets, open it and insert a couple of flat sachets of dry potpourri between the sheets. Seal the box with plastic wrap and leave it for three months before use.

### Lemon Verbena Ink

*1 handful dried lemon verbena*
*1 small bottle ink*

Stir the lemon verbena through the ink in a small, non-aluminium saucepan. Simmer for 45 minutes, adding 1 to 2 teaspoons of water, as desired. Strain, pressing the flowers down well in a fine sieve. Pour the scented ink back into the bottle.

## STATUES AND ORNAMENTS

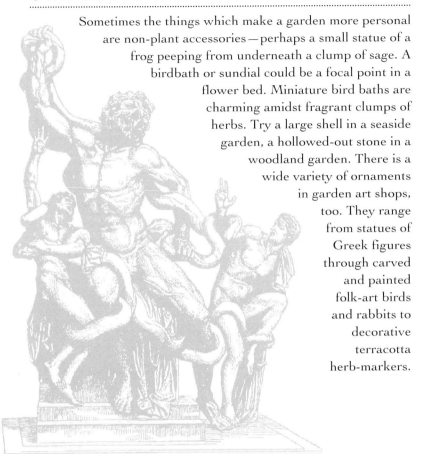

Sometimes the things which make a garden more personal are non-plant accessories—perhaps a small statue of a frog peeping from underneath a clump of sage. A birdbath or sundial could be a focal point in a flower bed. Miniature bird baths are charming amidst fragrant clumps of herbs. Try a large shell in a seaside garden, a hollowed-out stone in a woodland garden. There is a wide variety of ornaments in garden art shops, too. They range from statues of Greek figures through carved and painted folk-art birds and rabbits to decorative terracotta herb-markers.

## STRAWBERRIES

For optimum flavour (and this old wives' tale has been borne out in commercial production), incorporate scrapings of topsoil from below pines or spruces when preparing strawberry beds and, afterwards, mulch them with pine and spruce needles, crushed fir cones or splintered conifer twigs. If you have any of these trees in the garden, set strawberries about them.

Strawberries also make attractive edgings to paths and borders, especially the bushier Alpine varieties, such as 'Baron Solemacher', which form clumps. They are also very decorative in special terracotta or earthenware strawberry-planter pots, or in barrels pieced with holes. To set strawberries in a planter pot, first line the base with rocks or stones to facilitate drainage. Then gradually fill the pot with good quality potting mix, forking through some compost as you go. When each opening is reached, insert the strawberry plants from the *outside* and fill the top of the container with them as well. Allow the runners to hang down and root in the openings, instead of being supported, so they appear to climb.

Be careful to keep your strawberry planter well watered. The little pockets are notorious for drying out rapidly. A trick worth remembering, particularly for those likely to be absent from their gardens for long periods, is to set a pierced length of piping in the middle of the planter pot as you are filling it up with soil. Before going away on holidays, fill a narrow-necked bottle or flagon with water and wedge it, upended, over the mouth of the piping. It may look a little odd, but it will save your strawberries while you are away.

Strawberries thrive next to pyrethrum, an attractive plant with bright green leaves and small, yellow-centred flowers, well known as a natural insect repellent. Companion planting of strawberries with lavender is also recommended to those trying to deter birds during the fruiting season. Old wives say strawberry runners put forth larger fruit when borage is planted nearby. They also like to be close to beans, lettuce and spinach.

However, they turn away from soil where cabbages are planted; nor will they be happy if strong-scented rosemary, mint or thyme are too close. Gladioli are the kiss of death for strawberries — they'll die from the effect of these flowers even if they are planted at the other end of the garden.

Once picked, strawberries should be used as soon as possible because they perish so quickly. Unless the berries are very grubby, it is best to avoid washing them. Wiping them over with a damp cloth to remove dust or grit is the best way. Eat your freshly picked strawberries in fruit salads, by themselves with different toppings, in a refreshing sorbet between courses or in mousses, jams or pies. One of the simplest taste sensations is to dip fresh strawberries in natural yoghurt and then lightly dust each one with allspice — delicious! Or, try this:

## Strawberries and Fresh Coconut

In a chilled bowl, beat a quantity of cream and brown sugar until softly whipped. Fold in freshly grated coconut and a few drops of almond essence, to taste. Serve with strawberries which have been lightly sprinkled with grated nutmeg.

*See also Beans; Cabbages; Lavender; Lettuce*

IF BEES STAY AT HOME, RAIN WILL SOON COME;
IF BEES STAY AWAY, FINE WILL BE THE DAY.

## SUNBURN

To prevent heatstroke and sunburn, be sure to don a big, shady hat and avoid working the garden when the sun is directly overhead. Be wary of taking certain drugs, too. Tranquilisers and diuretics are notorious for creating photosensitive reactions with the sun, causing blotching and freckling of the skin. Ask your doctor about any pills you may have to take. Better still, see if the calming effect of hard work and fresh air doesn't enable you to do without (or at least cut down on) medication.

By the same token, never *ever* spray yourself with insecticides. They are not repellents and their toxic properties are absorbed through the skin. In addition, they can definitely cause rashes and other photosensitive reactions. Before you say you're far too smart to do this, let me say that I was stupid enough to do this once, when pestered to distraction by sandflies. Not smart at all.

WHEN HARVEST FLIES HUM
THERE'S WARM WEATHER TO COME.

Always apply a sunblock and remember vulnerable spots, like your neck and ears and the back of your legs. If you do suffer from sunburn, try a blend of equal parts of sour cream, yoghurt and buttermilk, straight from the fridge, to soothe overheated skin. Raw egg yolks, tomato and cucumber slices are all time-honoured remedies for taking the sting out of a carelessly-acquired sunburn. If you get a touch too much sun, reach for the vinegar bottle and take a good sniff. This works just as well as lavender smelling salts to overcome giddiness or nausea. Then take a good drink of water.

## SURPRISE PACKETS

Saving seeds from your flowers or vegetables can save you quite a lot of money. Plus, you avoid all the poisonous insecticides that many nurseries now use to dress their seed before sale.

Package up small envelopes of seed from your garden at the end of summer. You could name the herb or flower or, better still, leave it blank as a lucky dip for the recipient. Try clustering an assortment of such seed packages into a small gift basket, or pop them into the toes of Christmas stockings ... and remember, the gift will be even more appreciated if you include planting instructions.

SNAILIE, SNAILIE,

SHOOT OUT YOUR HORNS.

TELL US IF IT WILL BE A BONNIE DAY THE MORN.

(SCOTTISH PROVERB)

## TALKING TO PLANTS

Flowers, fruit and vegetables seem to inspire conversation. One friend, certain that plants respond to kindness and hate to be neglected, regularly walks through his garden encouraging the ailing and thanking the others for their beautiful blooms. Even professional gardeners find time for a chat. Pierre Philion of Quebec is recorded as having 3500 apple trees of his own and to care for 500,000 more in his job with the Department of Agriculture. He talks to them. All of them.

Conversations are brisk as often as they are sentimental. Maggie Bayliss, in her book *House Plants for the Purple Thumb*, falls back on a forthright 'Grow, damn you!'—much as Guernsey gardeners believed any herb grew the better for a stimulating curse at planting time.

## TANSY

Tansy was one of the strewing herbs used in the old days and it continues to be useful as an all-purpose insect repellent. Also known as 'bitter buttons' and 'scented fern', it should be planted in orchards to deter borers and flying insects. It is a good companion to roses, raspberries and grapes and, chopped up, is an excellent 'activator' for the compost heap.

*See also Ants; Aphids; Bookmarks; Fruit Growing; Moth Deterrents*

## TAMARILLOS

Tamarillos, or Brazilian tree tomatoes, are another garden staple which easily produce a frenzy of fruit. If you (and your neighbours) are overwhelmed with tamarillos, try making up large batches of this jam, which is another old church fête favourite.

### Tamarillo and Cinnamon Jam

*1½ kg (3½ lb) tamarillos*
*500 ml (16 fl oz) water*
*100 ml (3½ fl oz) apple cider vinegar*
*juice of 2 lemons*
*juice of 1 orange*
*1 cinnamon stick*
*1 teaspoon cloves*
*½ teaspoon powdered cinnamon*
*900 g (30 oz) white sugar*

Scald the tamarillos, then drain and skin the fruit. Chop roughly. Combine them with water, vinegar, powdered cinnamon, lemon and orange juices in large, non-aluminium saucepan. Place the cinnamon stick and cloves in a small, muslin spice bag, tie it securely and add it to the pan. Bring to the boil and simmer for 30 minutes, mashing the mixture against the sides of the pan. Remove the muslin spice bag, bring the pan to the boil again and add the sugar, stirring until it is dissolved. Boil rapidly for 45 minutes, or until it begins to gel. Spoon the jam into heated, sterile jars and cap them securely.

IF FROST COMES ON MORNINGS TWAIN,
THE THIRD DAY WE WILL SURELY HAVE RAIN.

THUNDER IN SPRING,
COLD IT WILL BRING.

WHEN EAGER BITES THE THIRSTY FLEA,
CLOUDS AND RAIN YOU'LL SHORTLY SEE.

## TEA LEAVES

My grandmother always took her tea pot religiously down the back steps and tipped the damp leaves around the base of the camellia bush. It rewarded her with hundreds of luscious, pink flowers each year, eventually growing to about 4 m (13 ft) high. So, when you have finished telling fortunes, save the tea leaves as a mulch for your camellias. Similarly, a tonic made from a little strong (cooled) tea should produce effective results.

## THISTLES

For those who are sure they have a 'black' rather than 'green' thumb, rest assured there are several 'weeds' worthy of encouragement — or so says superstition, anyway. The Scots, for instance, claim thistles are lucky, for, on one occasion, the Norsemen were attacking at night and one of them stood on a thistle. His pained cry alerted the Scots and since then they have regarded it as a favourable omen.

## THYME

Thyme was commonly used in gypsy cookery as a stuffing for poultry. Romany girls would place sprigs of thyme under their pillows to ward off nightmares. An infusion may also be used as a soothing gargle for a sore throat.

## TOMATOES

Tomatoes grow well with onions, nasturtiums and parsley. They will protect asparagus against asparagus beetle and are said to reduce the incidence of black spot amongst roses. Don't plant tomatoes by apricot trees or potatoes and, if you are still smoking,

wash your hands thoroughly before
working in the garden, for tomatoes are
very susceptible to tobacco-
transmitted diseases.

*See also Asparagus; Basil;
Cabbages; Marigold; Nettles;
Parsley*

## TOUCH WOOD

I think I must have been a dryad in
a previous life for I love trees so,
experiencing a real pang if one has to be pruned or
cut down. Ever since Eve, trees have been held in awe for their
magical powers or miraculous origins. When people 'touch wood'
to prevent misfortune, it is a relic of this customary respect shown
to the tree's guardian spirit. Many trees had medicinal properties
or sacred symbolism, while certain trees and their seeds or nuts
augured particularly well for matters of the heart.

Certain trees are also fairy homes. Humans foolish enough to
pass by one of these host-trees late at night may find themselves
inexplicably pinched or scratched, probably due to protective fairy
fingers. Willow trees are said to actually uproot themselves at
night and stalk, muttering, behind unwary travellers, according to
this very ancient poem:

*Ellum do grieve, oak he do hate
Willow do walk, if Yew travels late.*

Three hawthorn trees growing closely together are often haunted,
especially if the branches are twisted together. An oak, an ash and
a thorn tree growing close to each other are thought to be a
particularly potent combination, and a twig taken from each and
bound together with scarlet thread, then slipped under a nuptial
mattress, is an old Irish love-charm. However, as with all
fairy trees, they should be approached with considerable caution.
If in doubt, remember that the fairies love bright and pretty
things, so hang a haunted tree with ribbons or tinsel as
propitiatory gifts for them.

## TUBS

One of the most attractive inner-city gardens I've ever seen was a very small courtyard, covered with flagstones and decorated with large wooden tubs, spilling over with aromatic and colourful plants, flowers and herbs of every description. There were the silvery leaves of lavender, yellow and gold balm, bright geraniums and splashy, showy petunias. All were very bright and many retained their foliage throughout the year.

Before filling tubs with soil, set some broken pottery shards over the drainage holes, to stop the holes becoming clogged with wet soil. Mix a little powdered lime and mushroom compost with soil for the best result. Incidentally, some inner-city gardens contain too much sulphur and soot in their soils from days gone by, so it's best to use fresh soil for filling your tubs, rather than taking it from the yard.

When planting, try to arrange foliage to take advantage of contrasting colours. If, for instance, you want rosemary in the centre of your tub, plant lavender cotton (*Santolina incana*) and golden marjoram around the sides for added impact. Different varieties of the same plant, like the various sages, also look superb in a tub. Try planting several of the different sages — one type has very bright, red flowers, which are cheerful, and contrast with *Salvia officinalis* 'Purpurea', which has rich, plum-coloured leaves. There are also several varieties of lemon-scented thyme, including a silver-leafed one.

*See also Matches; Strawberries; Window Boxes*

# TUSSIE-MUSSIES

In earlier times, tiny bouquets of herbs and flowers were referred to as 'tussie-mussies' and they were carried to ward off germs and overcome the stench of less-than-adequately ventilated streets and homes. By the Victorian era, however, these pretty 'tussie-mussies' were more likely to be exchanged as lovers' troth-tokens and were valued for the sentiments or meanings attached to the various herbs and flowers. For example, pansies were named for the French *pensées* (thoughts) and mean 'I only think of your sweet face'. A red rosebud surrounded by forget-me-nots and southernwood signified undying devotion, remembrance and constancy. A bouquet of Christmas roses ('Please relieve my anxiety') and geraniums ('I miss you so') were certainly an urgent plea from the heart, though primroses (Inconstancy) and hydrangeas ('You are a coquette') could only be interpreted as a rebuff for a heartless flirt. Sage, with white and gold chamomile flowers, was emblematic of long life, wisdom and patience.

These are only a few of the meanings associated with various plants. When you make a tussie-mussie, arrange it in the traditional manner, placing the smaller leaves and flowers in concentric circles of contrasting colours around a central flower or large bud, like a camellia. Then edge it with ferns and silvery lambs' ears, tie it firmly with ribbon and write your message on a card, mentioning the significance of the bouquet you have assembled.

A sick friend will greatly appreciate a tussie-mussie—or use them as place cards or gifts.

A BAD GARDENER WILL QUARREL WITH HIS RAKE.

## VINEGARS

Flower-flavoured vinegars can be based on either apple cider vinegar or white wine vinegar. They are excellent with summer fruits and salads, especially melon and strawberries. They can be made very simply by packing fresh, scented flowers or leaves loosely into jars. Roses, violets and lavender all produce delicious vinegars. Borage flowers may be used, too, or small leaves from a lemon-, nutmeg- or spice-scented geranium. Then cover with vinegar, capping securely and letting the jar stand for a week or so, preferably in a sunny spot. At the end of that time, strain and rebottle the vinegar and store it in a cool place until needed.

Mint and lemon vinegar adds a fresh taste to salad dressings and is very simple to make. In summer, when they are their best, pick leaves of mint and of lemon-scented geranium. Wash and dry them (this is important; if they're not properly dried, the vinegar will cloud). Depending on the type and size of your bottle, use the leaves whole or chopped. Put several teaspoons of both mint and geranium leaves into each bottle, then fill with white wine or apple cider vinegar. Seal securely with a non-metallic lid and label.

## VIOLETS

It was the prophet Mohammed who said, '... as my religion is above all others, so is the excellence of the odour of violets above all others. It is warmth in winter and coolness in summer.' I must say I agree with his rather fulsome praise, for I love tiny, delicate violets, too.

Thoughts of innocence and romance come to mind when one thinks of violets. However, did you know that they are edible as well as ornamental? A wine made from sweet violets was popular in ancient times and violet vinegar, made by steeping the flowers in white wine vinegar, has a delicious scent and an absolutely beautiful colour. Violet tea, honey of violets, violet jubes, violet marmalade and violet cakes are all delectable recipes from bygone days. Crystallised or sugared violets are easy to prepare and add

an enchanting taste to spring desserts. You may also use this method to crystallise other edible flowers, such as roses or carnations:

## Crystallised Violets

*150 g (5 oz) Parma violets*
*1 to 2 egg whites, lightly whisked*
*caster sugar*

Using a small, soft paint brush or a make-up brush, paint the violets with egg white. Carefully dip the flowers in the sugar, sprinkling a little extra over where you have held them, to ensure an even coating (*Tip*: use tweezers). Place the violets on greaseproof paper, spread them on a wire rack and leave them in a warm place to dry until they are crisp. Turn them occasionally so they dry evenly. Crystallised violets may be stored in an airtight container, between layers of absorbent paper, for up to a week before use.

Violet leaves make an attractive base for holding moulds or jellies and the flowers may be used as a garnish for chilled fruit soups, with a dollop of sour cream. To make a violet salad, combine spinach and violet leaves with sliced, fresh, button mushrooms, water chestnuts, lemon juice, extra virgin olive oil and cayenne pepper. Crisp one cup of violet flowers in iced water, dry them and then arrange them on top of the salad.

*See also Holy Plants; Kidney Problems; Potpourri; Vinegars*

# WASTE NOT, WANT NOT

So say many old wives, and most good gardeners, for that matter. Use old egg cartons as punnet boxes, for instance. They're just the right size for seedlings and, if you wish, you can plant the whole carton or cut it up into plantlets, to save distributing tender new roots. Being cardboard, the cartons will rapidly break down in the soil and provide valuable moisture-retentive mulch. Never throw out old pantyhose. Plait or twist the legs together to make soft, pliable bindings for growing trees or for tying back thick masses of climbing vines. Unlike rope or string, the pantyhose will 'give' in windy weather, thus saving the plant from being broken or torn. Plastic yoghurt tubs are a terrific gardening tool as well. Either use them as seedling pots or inserts for planter boxes, or upturn them and use them as shields on stakes in the vegetable patch. Here they will actually have a dual purpose, helping to scare birds and also saving your eyes, for if you happen to bend over the unguarded tip of a wooden stake, it could cause terrible damage.

## WATER

Water the gardener, as well as the garden. Be sure to drink plenty of fluids when you are working hard in the garden. When you are down on all fours weeding the vegetable patch in summer, the near-ground temperature is likely to be at least 32°C (91°F). You'll need *at least* a litre of water every couple of hours to keep your body's systems correctly hydrated, more if you're on the heavy side.

## WINDOW BOXES

As long ago as 1594, Sir Hugh Platt wrote, 'In every window, you may make square frames ... of boards, well pitched within. Fill with some rich earth and plant such flowers and herbs therein as you like best.'

Where space is limited, window boxes are a terrific idea for

growing compact plants. Thyme, marjoram and winter savory, hyssop, dwarf white lavender and golden sage are all pretty choices for window boxes and, being evergreen, will remain colourful year-round. Want even more colour? Sow one or two dwarf geraniums with the herbs—the varieties with variegated or bronzed leaves are especially pretty.

Victorian-era windowboxes made from metal, with ornately worked patterns on the front, are much sought after by collectors. Failing this, it is a reasonably easy matter for you or a local carpenter to make a set from a wood that resists moisture, such as a hardwood or red cedar. Fill the box with fresh, fibrous loam, mixed with some generous handfuls of blood and bone. Spring is the best time to plant window boxes. Keep plants tidy by regularly pinching back new growth.

**TIP:** Window boxes dry out *very* rapidly, even if the weather is not particularly hot. A good idea is to fill a narrow-necked jar or bottle (an old wine flagon is ideal) with water, up-end it quickly and push it into the soil, between the plants. Tilt it very slightly until you see a few air bubbles rising, which means the water is seeping into the soil. It will take at least 3 days for the bottle to empty, making this a boon for gardeners going away for a weekend.

## WITCHES

When planting pretty foxgloves, don't place them too close to the front door, for witches slip the bell-like flowers onto their fingers so they may tamper with your locks. Chicory and ferns are unwise choices for the same reason, chicory being credited with the power to open doors and gates, while fern-seed renders thieves invisible. The Scots say bracken is the only exception to this rule, for Jesus Christ blessed it and any household where it grew would be kept safe in His name. Proof of this is found on the underside of the leaves. Each one is marked with an 'x', the symbol for Christ and for *chi*, which is the 22nd letter of the Greek alphabet.

In medieval times, marjoram was considered a powerful charm against witchcraft. Both the mysterious mugwort and the more common plantain were credited with clasping a magic coal in their roots, which protected any house nearby from thunder, attack by wild beasts or disease. St John's Wort is even more efficacious against spells, for it provides actual protection against evil fairies and witches. Being a sun symbol, like the daisy, St John's Wort was much used in pagan midsummer festivals and is both a powerful protection and a healing plant.

*See also Caraway Charm; Elder; Ghost Busters*